HOW I LEARNED TO

SHOOT 75, OCCASIONALLY

— *A FANATIC'S APPROACH TO GOLF*

DEDICATION: To all who hate to love this incredible game of golf. Especially to the members of my regular golfing groups who helped me improve and provided so many hours of enjoyment.

Special thanks to each and everyone who provided support and encouragement.

By Barry Ceminchuk

i

ISBN 0 646 13115 X

FIRST EDITION

Published by OZ IT

P.O. Box 51047
6525 - 118 Avenue
Edmonton Alberta T5W 5G5
Canada

Cover Design by Powerpro Computer Solutions Ltd.

Typesetting and printing by
Art Design Printing Inc., Edmonton, AB, Canada

Book Binding by A-1 Bindery Services Ltd.

TABLE OF CONTENTS

PREFACE

This book will not teach you how to hit a golf ball, it will teach you how I learned to score.

This book will not teach you how to shoot 63, it will teach you how I learned to shoot 75, occasionally.

This book is aimed at the amateur golfer struggling with their game. It is designed to fill the gap between the beginning golfer and the touring professional.

This book explains the stages I went through and the knowledge gained as I improved my handicap from 19 to 5, and learned to shoot in the 70's.

If you are a social golfer who plays the game as an alternative to a walk in the park, this book is not for you.

If you just like to hit a golf ball and do not spend any time planning your shots, this book may not be for you.

If you enjoy the game and would one day like to play at a higher level, this book may be for you.

If you are presently at a level where you feel you should be improving but are not, this book is probably for you.

If you are always looking for ideas and constantly adapting these ideas to your golf game, this book is for you.

If you have set yourself a personal goal of gaining the knowledge and ability to shoot 75, this book is definitely for you.

CHAPTER 1
INTRODUCTION

WHAT DO I DO NOW? HOW DO I LOWER MY HANDICAP?
These questions, asked by a member of my golfing group, started a discussion that gave me the idea for this book. The points covered and the conclusions we came to were:

1.	PLAY EVERY DAY. None of us had the available time. We had work, family commitments, home maintenance, etc. It was all we could do to play a few times a week.
2.	PRACTICE FREQUENTLY. Again not enough time. Besides, we did not enjoy spending hours hitting balls. Most of us did practice every couple of weeks or so, but this was as often as we wanted. We also knew there was more to the game than just hitting a golf ball.
3.	TAKE LESSONS. Excellent for learning the swing mechanics and the basics of the game, but after these are learned a person must improve on their own. We all had seen many spend a lot of money on lessons and practice endlessly, but still not be able to score well.
4.	ATTEND A GOLF SCHOOL. None of us had been to one or knew anyone who had; therefore we could not comment.
5.	READ INSTRUCTION BOOKS AND MAGAZINE ARTICLES. Some are very good, but the vast majority are aimed at either the beginning golfer and teach the swing mechanics or they explain the game from the perspective of the touring professional who shoots in the 60's. There is a large gap here.
	We all knew the swing mechanics and agreed they were impor-tant but we also knew we would never have the ability to hit the ball and play at the level of the professionals. We just wanted to know how to improve our game. We were in the gap.
6.	VIDEO'S. Again, some are very good but basically they contain the same material as the books, they just use moving images instead of still pictures to illustrate the points. They have the same weaknesses as the books.

After these comments we all agreed the available instructional information was good, but insufficient to meet our specific needs. We also agreed we did not have the time, or want to make the effort to improve our games the traditional way.

1

Thinking over these points sometime later, I decided if I ever managed to get my handicap down to a low number I would write a book and explain how I did it. This is the result.

This book explains how I personally learned, and it was a lengthy learning process, to shoot 75, occasionally.

The main purpose of this book is to explain the stages I went through and the knowledge gained from the prospective of a fanatical amateur golfer struggling to improve his game. By showing you the reader the problems I encountered and the answers I found, I hope you will learn from my experience, increase your speed of improvement and enhance your enjoyment of this game.

There are two ways to view the points within this book. The first is to wonder "Who is this guy (the author) and ask why should I listen to him?" The second is to look at what this guy says and ask "What can I learn from the information presented?"

This book is aimed at the people with the second attitude. The material discusses how one average guy improved his game by using a little thought and common sense. An average guy who does not hit the ball great, or long and does not have the time to perfect his game.

I show what I have learned and allow the reader to judge whether each point is appropriate for them. This overcomes the major flaw of telling people what to do, which may or may not be right for them. There are many ways to play the game and each person must choose what is best for them.

The early chapters discuss the main points that contributed to my improvement during specific stages, and the later chapters discuss the issues which I feel were most important, in greater detail.

The topics covered are:

- The author's background.
- The specific stages I went through and the major factors that allowed me to improve to the next stage.
- The issues to consider when choosing a home course.
- The factors to review when selecting the proper equipment.
- The all important mental aspects, including confidence, concentration, discipline, temperament and gamesmanship.
- The effect different weather conditions can have on you and your game.
- The methodology I use to make at least 90 percent of my short putts.

- The recurring swing problems that regularly appear in my game, along with my remedies.
- The checklists and routines I have developed over the years. These include warmup, pre-shot and practice routines.
- The concept of course management. This concept is illustrated by a hole-by-hole analysis demonstrating the issues I faced when playing my home course. Trouble shots and factors to consider when playing a strange course are also covered.
- A potpourri of short topics including taking advantage of the rules, lessons, unusual hints, and a few golf stories.
- A list of the main points as a quick reference.

The points and tips discussed go beyond anything I have read. I feel they will benefit anyone who is serious about the game. I do not profess to have all the answers; I just know what has worked for me.

Many sections of this book present detailed sequences and issues to be analyzed. At first reading they may seem overwhelming. In my case I have acquired this knowledge and developed these routines over many years, I just keep adding a little at a time.

I suggest you read them through the first time and not try to memorise them completely. Then go back and select the points you feel will help you improve the most. Concentrate on integrating this selected subset into your present game.

When you are comfortable with your subset you can then refer back and select a new subset. Over time the knowledge in this book will become as familiar to you as it is to me.

Some of the issues I discuss may on the surface seem trivial. I include these details to show the preparation I go to in order to reduce the problems I may have on the course. Poor off-course preparation will affect on-course performance. Being properly prepared to play by paying attention to the appropriate details helps eliminate distractions with minor issues and allows me to focus on playing the game.

There is also a lot of information here. Remember golf is very difficult and it takes years to learn how to play it properly. This is what makes it so addicting and keeps us coming back.

In this book I discuss specific problems I had with certain holes on my home course. As you the reader will probably never see these holes I suggest you concentrate on the playability factors being discussed and try think of similar situations on the course you play most often.

To measure my progress in the game of golf I used my handicap as the yardstick. The stages I went through were:

STAGE 1:	Handicap 19 to 16	3 Seasons
STAGE 2:	Handicap 16 to 13	1 Season
STAGE 3:	Handicap 13 to 10	2 Seasons
STAGE 4:	Handicap 10 to 7	3 Seasons
STAGE 5:	Handicap 7 to 5	2 Seasons

The number of seasons required within each stage is dependent on the individual starting skill level and physical and mental attributes. What is shown here is the number of seasons it took me to advance to the next stage. More dedication in the early stages and perhaps the contents of this book will allow some to considerably shorten the timeframe.

I selected the handicap groupings based on what I found to be a common level of skill. From stage to stage there were differences in my ability, my concerns, my attitude and the areas that I worked on.

I consider a stage to end when a major improvement in my game and ability to score became apparent. This is very subjective and arbitrary. Others may have different groupings.

The points covered were fairly universal among the golfers I played with regularly. We seemed to develop at a similar rate and these were the issues we discussed after a round.

By showing you the issues I faced and the growth path I chose, I hope to help you better choose your own.

To improve one's golf game requires dedication and some time. If you are not seriously willing to spend the time and effort required, you can only expect a marginal improvement, if any at all. The time and effort is not the same as that needed to play at the level of the professionals, but a commitment is required.

Above all a person must enjoy playing golf. If you do not enjoy it, do not play the game. It will frustrate you to a point of exasperation and quite possibly shorten your life.

Also, in order to improve you must assess the strengths and weaknesses of your game and determine a realistic level of expectation. Do not delude yourself.

I used to think through a completed round and tell myself IF this or that did not happen I would have shot 69. I don't believe in IF any more. IF my ball would have bounced the other way after it hit that tree, IF I would not have three putted those greens, IF I would not have hit those bad shots and so on. I stopped this thinking.

I have never had a round where everything went perfectly my way. I have had some rounds where I played very well, and received more good breaks than bad, but never all good. This is part of the game and I accept it. The only thing that counts is the score at the end of the round. There is no such thing as a round with IF in it; there is only the score.

It is ironic I once thought if I could get my handicap into single digits I would be ecstatic. When I got there I wanted to be able to answer the question "What is your handicap?" by holding up one hand. Now I can do that, I want it to be lower. I do however rationalize my not improving to the next stage by telling myself the sacrifice to attain this would be too much. Therefore I am happy, well almost happy, and I accept it.

The ability to shoot 75 occasionally is an acceptable level. Jack Nicklaus and Greg Norman may not agree, but I am sure there are millions of golfers out there who do.

75 Occasionally

CHAPTER 2
HISTORY AND ENVIRONMENT

In order for you the reader to understand my approach to the game, some historical and environmental information is in order. I was born in Edmonton Alberta, Canada. I started to play golf relatively seriously at the age of 23. Prior to this I played three to five times per year and only then on social occasions.

When I became interested in golf I searched for others who were also interested in the game. At that time I played fifteen times over the summer. With one exception, these games were all on public courses. The exception was a round on the private course, Highlands Golf Club. The next year a friend was able to get me into the club as a member. I was on my way as a serious golfer.

Highlands is a 6,408 yard (5859 metre) course which plays to a par of 71. The course is situated in an old river valley with the river as the southernmost boundary. The overall terrain is hilly and it would be classified as a parkland course (as opposed to links).

Highlands has hosted qualifying rounds for regional professional tournaments and held a number of serious amateur tournaments. Although the members may not like to hear this, it is probably not the best course in Edmonton, but in my opinion, it is one of the better courses. It never seems to play the same from day to day, and most holes are easy bogeys but not easy pars or birdies. Personally I like the golf course.

When discussing golf in Edmonton, Canada, the climate must be understood. In the winter there is snow on the ground and temperatures can reach 40 Degrees below zero — a little too cold for golf. The golf season usually starts in April and ends in October. I consider the serious season to start in May and end in September if the weather is good enough.

Playing golf in a place like Edmonton has a number of advantages and disadvantages. The main advantage is the daylight hours. As Edmonton is so far north, approximately 54 degrees latitude, there is a lot of daylight in summer. In June you can play to 11 P.M. and in May and September you can usually play until 8:45 P.M.

This allows one to play golf after work without special sacrifices like taking vacation time or time off without pay. To play golf reasonably well you must play frequently.

The other advantage is also a disadvantage — the short season. The advantageous point is the time and dedication needed to maintain a proper golf game is only required for a portion of the year. I am convinced I cannot maintain the full commitment required for me to play reasonably well, all year round.

The disadvantage of the short season is the winter lay-off has a number of detrimental affects on one's golf game. The most obvious is the loss of "touch", especially with the short game which occurs when one does not play often. The mental sharpness also tends to go "flat" and the keenness and enthusiasm wanes. The enthusiasm can be regenerated but the "flatness" is hard to recover. I also experience a sense of frustration in the spring waiting for the course to open.

Another disadvantage of playing in Edmonton is the variation in the weather. This makes the game very difficult to learn. The temperature range can be quite significant, even on the same day. For example, at 7 a.m. on a summer day, the temperature may only be 39 Degrees Fahrenheit (4 Degrees Celsius) and by noon it may be into the 70's (20's Celsius). In the spring and fall it may be below freezing and warm up to the 60's or 70's (10's or 20's Celsius). Or it may be cold in the morning and only warm up a few degrees all day.

In other words to play golf well in Edmonton, one has to know how to handle differences in weather conditions not only from day to day but even within a round.

The other disadvantage is the damage done to the course during the winter. With a good greens superintendent and some luck with the snowfall and thawing patterns, the course may come out of a winter with only average damage. The damage which does occur shows up as winterkill. This is patches of dead grass varying in size from a few inches (centimetres) to sizeable sections of the course.

On the fairways the winterkill results in the ball frequently sitting down on dirt with tufts of grass in front of and behind the ball. This makes a shot difficult to control, even for the better players. Around the green it can make a chip shot or flip wedge shot extremely tricky if not impossible.

On the greens winterkill can be an even bigger problem. Having to putt through the holes can cause the ball to bounce and be deflected offline. For some reason my putts rarely get deflected in the right direction. Trying to judge speed and direction on damaged greens can be very difficult.

In the early part of the season when players are trying to rebuild and refamiliarize themselves with all aspects of their game, the effect of winterkill has a major impact on one's progress and confidence unless one is aware of, and allows for it.

That is the environment in which I learned to play golf. I have recently been living in Australia, first Sydney and then Melbourne, and found the playing conditions somewhat different. The knowledge I have gained from playing there is reflected in the points discussed.

Regarding my physical environment, I am 5 feet 8 inches tall (173 centimetres) and my weight is 165 pounds (75 kilograms). I have played some sports at an amateur level but am not overly athletic.

I am what I call a fanatical person. Once I become interested in something, I get very involved in the subject. This fanatical personality was a direct factor in my having the desire to improve, and helped me achieve the improvements.

As for intelligence, well that is a matter for debate. My occupation is data processing professional.

After graduation from college I spent a number of years in the Information Technology industry within the IBM mainframe environment. My job roles have included programmer, systems analyst, systems programmer, planner, manager and sales representative. The companies I have worked for include a large utility, small computer consulting firms and a vendor of large mainframe computers. I have also worked independently as a freelance consultant.

I state these in order for you the reader to understand my background and approach to the game of golf. The companies I have worked for and the job roles I have performed, as well as all my experiences in life have led me to this approach. As a data processing person, my approach to the game of golf is similar to my approach to my working environment.

75 Occasionally

CHAPTER 3
THE MYTH OF SCORING

Before we get into the specific stages, some comments on scoring. Many golfers believe to score well they must make a lot of birdies, eagle the par 5's, hit the ball 300 yards (270 metres) off the tee and their wedge 130 yards (120 metres). This is a myth.

You simply do not have to do that. I have seen many players who hit the ball 200 to 210 yards (180 to 190 metres) off the tee, do not make many birdies, rarely make an eagle and still manage to have a single digit handicap.

These players keep the ball in play and rarely make double bogeys. Their short game is good and they play position golf. They try to place their shots in the position which gives them the easiest next shot. They may not hit a lot of great shots but they hit very few bad shots. Always in play, not spectacular. "Steady Eddie" is usually their nickname.

For all holes Eddie tries to be on or around the green in regulation strokes. Regulation is one shot for a par 3, two for a par 4, etc. From on or around the green Eddie depends on his short game to get the ball in the hole for a par or bogey, with an occasional birdie. With a reasonable short game, from this position a double bogey should be next to impossible.

The only acceptable reason for taking more than three shots from on or around the green is a bad break like being against the lip of a bunker. Otherwise the worst Eddie should make is bogey. Double bogeys then become rare and triple bogeys unheard of.

If Eddie can hit an occasional (maximum) tee shot 230 yards (207 metres) and his 3 wood 200 yards (180 metres) including roll, he has an effective range of 430 yards (390 metres). For a par 4 this is long by any standards and there are seldom more than four holes of this length or longer on any course, even championship courses.

On the few longer par 4 holes, Eddie should have no more than a short wedge shot to the green. This assumes there are no long carries over water and if there are, most holes have a bailout or safe area that can be played to. If he has a reasonable short game he should be able to wedge on and two putt, with an occasional one putt. Therefore he will make no worse than bogey and possibly a one putt par.

Eddie may have trouble with a few long par 3's, but if he plays them smart he makes no worse than bogey. If he bogeys four long par 4's and two long par 3's he is 6 over. If he can make two or three birdies on the short holes he has a very good score. Even if he gets a couple of bogeys on the remaining holes his score is still under 80.

Start shooting around 80 consistently and you will occasionally have a very good game where you shoot a few shots better. Chip in a couple times, make a couple of long putts, maybe even get a hole-in-one (stretching this point, I know) and you will find yourself occasionally shooting around the mid 70's.

I bring up Eddie as an example of one way to approach the game. Even if you are a power player who hits the ball long, the basic funda-mentals of scoring are the same. Keep the ball in play and get the ball in the hole in as few shots as possible. Distance can be an advantage as long as it is controlled. Out of control, distance is a major liability.

I am not suggesting you must play this way. Eddie's style may not be the type of game for which you are suited. It certainly does not fit most people's concept of a professional golfer, although some professionals play a high-level version of this type of game. You must analyze your own strengths and weaknesses and make your own decision as to how you are going to play. If your goal is to get into the single digit handicap range this is one way of getting you there.

So much for the myth of the big hitter making 8 birdies and 2 eagles every round. If you want to shoot 63 then yes you must make the birdies, but if you want to shoot 75 occasionally you do not.

Sounds simple does it not? I know, easier said than done. But worth thinking about.

Another point is the number of shots required to get around the course. On the par 4's you must hit the ball twice (unless playing a very short hole), on par 5's three times and on par 3's once to get the ball onto the green. Then you must hit a number of putts.

When you try to reduce your overall score there are some shots, no matter how well they are hit, that cannot be eliminated. So to improve your scoring you only have a limited number of ways to do it. Making more birdies is one way, but so is reducing the number of bogeys and double bogeys. A shot saved is a shot saved no matter where it is saved.

CHAPTER 4
STAGE 1: 19 to 16

In the following chapters I discuss the stages I went through and what I feel were the main points that allowed me to improve to the next stage.

During each stage I increased my knowledge and improved in a number of areas, but only a little at a time. To discuss each small improvement and piece of information would be too disjointed and not communicate the ideas effectively. Instead, I have chosen to present the highlights within each stage and discuss the major topics in detail in the chapters that follow.

Stage 1 lasted three seasons. It started when I joined the Highlands Golf Club. After the first month my handicap was 19.

Starting at this level was mainly due to the work I had done in the past and my enthusiasm. I had learned some things from the people I had been playing with and read a number of golf magazines as well as an instruction book. These gave me a basic understanding of the fundamentals of the game.

When I joined the club the first change was my attitude on the course. The rounds became games of golf, not social occasions. I was not out for a walk in the park but to actually play the game. I was trying to learn something new (how to play well) and realized this required all my effort.

I must admit at the time I was not proud of my golf game and was very careful with whom I played. I avoided golfers who were significantly better than I because I did not want to hold them up and affect their scores. I had to learn to play with others before I could feel comfortable enough to concentrate on my own game. This basically includes following etiquette, not talking too much and not playing too slowly. When I was able to concentrate on my own game I was able to improve. This is one of the reasons this stage lasted so long and my handicap did not drop quickly.

When my handicap was 19 my main areas of weakness were full shots especially the driver, and a very poor short game. I also had some basic swing problems and was not setting up to the ball properly.

With my driver, I was abysmal. Of the 14 drives per round, I doubt half would go more than 50 yards (metres) and the others would most likely have a big slice and end up in the trees. I spent many hours on the practice range trying to fix the problem but was not successful. My eventual solution was to use my 3 wood off the tee.

The message here is should you have a club you cannot hit, leave it in the bag. There is no real stigma here; many good players do this. If you are really concerned about it, search around for a club that meets your specifications. Or simply try different clubs until you find one you like the feel and look of, and can at least hit reasonably well.

Looking back, I now believe I was using a driver that was not right for me. It was too long and had too flexible a shaft. At that time I did not know enough to question the equipment I was using. I simply assumed any problems I had were due to my lack of skill. This is not always the case.

My second major area of weakness was my short game. I improved this by playing more frequently and practising flip wedge shots, chip shots and long putts approximately once a month.

I am lucky enough to have reasonably good "touch" for the shots which require this touch. Specifically, this touch is the ability to judge the force required to hit a partial shot the correct distance and the physical capability to execute the shot with the proper force.

Without this touch I do not believe I could have improved more than a little. Over time this touch has improved with practice and play. I believe this touch can be learned to a certain extent but there must be some natural talent there to begin with.

Another major factor that helped me improve was a group of lessons from the club professional. I took five lessons over a period of three weeks and also included a playing lesson.

The professional taught me the fundamentals of the golf swing. This included the grip, stance, address, posture and swing plane. He made a number of changes to my swing and setup. After every lesson I wrote down what I was taught and reviewed the notes regularly.

I spent a lot of time working on the changes he made. I knew my golf swing needed to be fundamentally correct and I concentrated on integrating these changes so they became automatic. I did have some problems initially, but after a few practice sessions the new swing and setup worked better than my old swing and setup.

Learning the fundamentals and applying them to my own particular physical characteristics provided me with a base for a reasonable golf swing. Not perfect by any means, but reasonable. This is an important point, I cannot emphasize it enough. I had to have this base before I could improve.

The regular lessons were excellent but I enjoyed the playing lesson more. The professional played 18 holes with me (this lesson is usually only 9 holes) and taught me to think about the position for my next shot while planning my current shot.

I must admit I did not really begin to spend a lot of time thinking about these course management issues until the later stages. At this time I was more concerned with hitting the ball reasonably well and learning the basics of playing the game.

I do however give the professional credit for his approach. He was trying to introduce me to the other aspects of the game. I was not yet knowledgeable enough to recognize this and work on these areas, but he had brought them up.

Another area I worked on was my complete address routine. I had read all good golfers have a pre-shot routine and go through it prior to every shot. I began to develop my own individual routine.

I did have one problem with the alignment portion of my routine. Initially, I would address the ball and do my final alignment to the target by turning my head and looking at the pin or aiming point. I became convinced there were two faults with this.

The first was I do not have the physical capability to correctly line up the face of a club to a target in the distance. I was sure that I was subconsciously aware of and subsequently correcting my misalignment during the swing. At times I could feel myself changing the direction of the swing during the actual swing. This caused all kinds of problems.

This was remedied by a tip in a golf magazine that suggested a person line up to a mark on the ground a short distance in front of the ball. I began to use this procedure and have kept with it ever since. I am absolutely convinced it helps me to line up properly.

The second fault with my alignment procedure related to my wearing glasses. When I turned my head to look at the target I was actually looking through the side and curved portion of the lenses. The curved portion distorted my view of the target.

I picked this up when I had a problem making putts. I kept hitting putts left of the hole and could not figure out why. While talking to a fellow who makes lenses for glasses, he mentioned there would be some distortion of the position of objects unless I was careful to look directly through the center of the lens. The distortion had created a false hole position and I was putting to this false position.

The solution was to ignore the false hole and putt over a mark on the ground. I also turned my head fully and kept my eyes aligned with the center of the lenses when I looked at the hole.

To counter the distortion for my full shots I developed a unique routine, described in Chapter 15 Section 15.1 FULL SHOT ROUTINE. Basically the procedure involves placing one hand out with fingers extended in line with my eyes and the target. I then bring the hand down, ensuring I follow the hand with my eyes in the center of the lenses, until the hand intersects with a point on the ground. The point on the ground is the spot I align to.

My procedure appears similar to a person praying and people thought I was praying before every shot. Many made jokes about this but I did not mind, I felt it was helpful to my game.

These small changes to my address routine helped ensure I was aligning properly. If I am not aiming at the target I cannot hit the ball there.

In the second season of this stage I increased my number of rounds to between 35 and 40 per season. I found a regular group to play with and this helped me get onto the course more frequently. During the first season I played occasionally with a few people but usually went to the course by myself and joined a group.

When I started playing more frequently I began to experience certain side effects that were due to fatigue and muscle weakness. If I played too often in a short time my hands, arms and legs became sore. This indicates my physical shape was not good and was a contributing factor to my not playing well.

In the third season of this stage I entered an elimination match play tournament that had flights based on handicap. The winners of each flight from the participating clubs got together for a one round Provincial Championship tournament. In Canada, Alberta is a province as opposed to a state.

When my handicap was 19 I was a tough competitor. I seemed to be able to scrape together a lot of pars and bogeys (without handicap strokes). I did however make a lot of triple bogeys. Still this made me very hard to beat in match play.

After a number of very difficult matches I won my flight. In one match I managed to shoot a gross score of 37 on the back nine. This caused some grumbling about my handicap being too high.

At first I felt guilty, but after I thought about it I knew my handicap was valid and I just happened to get lucky when I shot the 37. This was a personal best for me until then. I also had the thought that any time someone thinks I am a better player than my handicap indicates, I am happy.

Having won the flight entitled me to play in the Championship tournament. This was a big deal to me. I prepared for this tournament by playing almost every day for a month. The result was that by tournament day my handicap was down to 16, the lowest it had ever been.

On the day before the tournament we were allowed a practice round on the course. I had not played the course before and it was pouring rain. I mean hard rain. I picked up so many times I have no idea what general area my score was in. Far too high though.

It is interesting I did not let this bad round bother me. I just figured it was due to the bad weather and I was confident I would play better the next day. From the comments some of my team members made I am sure they were not as confident as I. I took the attitude that I was the high handicapper and if I played bad that was to be expected. If I played well, then great.

On tournament day I did not play the best of the group but I held my end up. Two of the other members did better than I and the third about the same. We tied for second and the prizes I received included a new golf bag and some balls. I enjoyed it immensely.

I mention this story because the whole experience of winning the matches and playing reasonably well in the tournament had a major impact on my confidence. I now really and truly believed I could become a better player. This renewed my hope and increased my enthusiasm. This enthusiasm was so strong it gave me solace when I was playing poorly over the next two seasons.

The other factor that helped was I occasionally played golf with a fellow at work who had once been a 5 handicap. He was very knowledgeable in all aspects of the game. Every chance I had I spent time talking golf with him, many times to the detriment of work. He taught me a lot. I remember he used to joke how I could still have a high handicap after all he had taught me.

The main factors that allowed me to lower my handicap from 19 to 16 were using my 3 wood instead of my driver off the tee, winning my flight and playing more often. The other factors I have mentioned all contributed but these are the main ones.

It is again worth mentioning I spent a lot of time learning the fundamentals of the golf swing (grip, address, etc.) and applied these fundamentals to create a somewhat reasonable swing. I learned these fundamentals and how to apply them to my physical characteristics from the golf professional. I could not improve until I had done this.

At the end of this stage I was very comfortable playing to a handicap of 16. I enjoyed playing in club tournaments because I was rarely far off this handicap and always felt I was contributing to the team.

75 Occasionally

CHAPTER 5
STAGE 2: 16 to 13

Stage 2 lasted one season. During Stage 1, I improved most aspects of my game and had been playing for a few seasons. I was now past the point of learning the basics.

By far the biggest factor in my improvement in this stage was due to playing more frequently and more regularly than in the past. I played 60 games, averaging three a week.

Playing this often resulted in major improvements to all aspects of my game but most notably my wedge game. My wedge shots, and all short game shots became more accurate through hitting them more often. My touch improved with regular play. Compared to my level during Stage 1, my short game improved approximately 100 percent.

I believe the vast majority of the shots I took off my handicap during this stage were due to this improvement with my short game. Even without the other issues I mention here, my handicap would still have dropped. The short game shots are the scoring shots and as they improve, so do the scores.

At this level they are critical. As I was not hitting a lot of greens in regulation and frequently getting in trouble, the better my short game became, the less impact the mediocre shots had on my score. I was able to increase the number of times I saved a par or a bogey.

Early in this stage I again analysed my tee shots. I was still using my 3 wood off the tee and was not happy about it. I felt I was giving away distance that I needed to score better. On some holes I needed the extra distance just to reach the green, especially in cold and wet conditions.

To solve this I decided to purchase a new set of woods. A set with a driver I could hit at least reasonably well. After some searching I found a set I liked and bought it. I used my new driver off the tee and it worked better than my previous driver, although still not as well as I had hoped.

With the driver I also started to hit a high draw shot. This was by choice and not due to the new driver. Prior to this my natural shot had been a fade, sometimes a slice. I decided to hit a draw because a number of people convinced me that to play well one had to hit a high draw off the tee. They believed this was the only way to play the game. I no longer believe this, but I did at the time.

Also during this stage I became extremely careful in determining distances to the green. When I was unsure of the distance, while I was making the swing I would be thinking whether to hit the ball hard or soft or if I had the correct club. These thoughts would occupy my mind and I believe, affect the quality of my shot. Knowing the correct distance allowed me to be confident I had the right club and therefore put a better swing on the ball.

Knowing the distance also eliminated the effect of the optical illusions the course architect had created. These included dips and mounds in front of a green that made the pin appear closer than it really was. Again, allowing me to be confident I had the right club.

I determined the distances I hit each of my clubs by noting the results of my shots during my rounds. I conducted a study, simply watching where my ball landed and doing a quick calculation of the distance the ball had flown. I was careful to only watch shots I hit at least reasonably well.

When I started this study I found most shots were not going as far as I thought. I then made adjustments to my expected distance for each club. I calculated a minimum and a maximum and frequently used the minimum distance for club selection, especially when there was a hazard to be carried.

I also became very conscious of the effect the elevation of the terrain (elevated greens for example) had on my shots. Again, by watching the results I was able to calculate the effect. This took almost the whole season before I was comfortable I had this figured out.

At this time I only made minor adjustments in my club selection due to the weather. I did the same study for these conditions in the next stage.

Before I could determine the distance I was getting with each club I needed to have a map of the course. Fortunately another member had taken measurements of each hole to landmarks, trees, bunkers, etc. and was kind enough to give his measurements to me. I thank him for this.

If you are serious about reducing your handicap I recommend you obtain a map of your course. If one is not available, measure it yourself.

A big factor that helped me improve during this stage was I began to keep detailed statistics of my performance on my home course. I kept statistics on the following. Greens in regulation — my low was 2 and my high was 9, average around 5 to 6. Total putts per round — low of 32 high of 42, average around 36. Number of drives in the fairway (out of 14) — low of 4, high of 12, average around 9. At this time I counted a drive ending up between the tree lines as in the fairway which included the longer contoured fairway. The number of shots to get the ball in the hole from within 140 yards (125 metres) from the middle of the green — low 2, high 6, average around 3.8. The number of birdies, pars, bogeys and others (more than bogey) per round — erratic numbers here, averages were less than one birdie per round, 5 or 6 pars, 8 or 9 bogeys, and 3 or 4 others. I recorded these statistics after every round and calculated averages every couple of weeks. They were a good indication of my ability at the time. As I improved these numbers improved.

Just keeping track of these statistics helped me identify problem areas. When I did poorly, I immediately analysed the cause of the poor result. This allowed me to focus on the true cause while it was still fresh in my mind. Previously, I would just go by the impression I was left with when I thought about it sometime later. Impressions are frequently wrong.

At the end of this stage I was more conscious of course management. The two principles I was utilising were placing the ball in a proper position for the next shot and choosing my target area for an approach based on the distance from the green.

Off the tee I tried to place my drives in the best position for the approach to the green or, on a par 5, the best position for my second shot. I worked backwards from the pin placement and allowed for hazards and playing conditions.

For approach shots I developed a rule of thumb for the target I would choose. If I was more than 140 yards (125 metres) away from the middle of the green I would aim for the safest area to reach (the area with the largest margin for error away from hazards) and was happy if the ball ended up on or near the green. From 100 to 140 yards (90 to 125 metres) I tried to hit the middle of the green. From less than 100 yards (90 metres) I became aggressive, trying to get the ball close to the pin.

I based these ranges on my skill level at that time. I have since changed my ranges to more than 180 yards (165 metres) to aim for the safest area, 150 to 180 yards (135 metres to 165 metres) to land in the middle of the green and less than 150 yards (135 metres) to shoot at the pin. As I improved I gradually lengthened the range for each type of approach.

I believe implementing these principals saved me shots and directly contributed to my handicap dropping. Instead of shooting for tight pin positions from long distances and ending up in a bunker or worse, I frequently ended up on the green or with an easy chip shot. These principles did not save me a shot every hole or every round, but gradually my scores started to improve.

By the end of this stage I was beginning to understand the object of the game of golf is not just to hit the ball well, but to play a sequence of shots, all of which get the ball in the hole in as few strokes as possible.

The next shot is dependent upon the previous shot. If the previous shot puts you in a good position the next shot becomes easier and has a higher probability of success.

For handicap golfers this is especially important. Because they have a higher probability of hitting a mediocre shot, the larger margin for error increases the probability of a reasonable result.

I also began to search for ideas about golf. After reading a large number of articles and books I concluded there was a lot of contradictory information written about the game. I actually reached a point where I was confused about which way I should be swinging and how I should play a number of shots. For example, I would read how one player handled a certain situation and then in another article, I would read that another player handled the same situation differently.

In a discussion with my playing partners they convinced me I had to understand my own game and choose the one way to play that was best for me, and me alone. The players in the magazines were doing exactly that. This was valuable advice. I had been listening to too many people and reading too many tips, trying to include them all in my game. A common but major mistake.

My playing partners also pointed out I was trying to play the game like the professionals, hit the ball long, make many eagles and birdies, have a perfectly repeatable swing, etc. Another mistake.

I then accepted my game for what it was, trying to attain improvements in areas I felt I could improve but not to apply everything I read or emulate the professionals.

At the end of this stage I was comfortable with a handicap of 13. I felt I could play to it and there was still room to improve. The issues and factors I have mentioned all contributed to my handicap dropping but the biggest single factor was the improvement in my short game due to playing more often. The short game is critical at this level.

As my short game improved I was able to save more pars and bogeys after a bad or mediocre shot. As I saved more pars and bogeys my scores went down. As my scores went down so did my handicap.

CHAPTER 6
STAGE 3: 13 to 10

Stage 3 lasted two seasons. A number of factors contributed to my improvement in this stage. Basically I was starting to analyse my game more and simply improving the way I hit the golf ball. I was playing better and smarter.

Reading two books was of immense value to me. The books are in the PLAY BETTER GOLF series, Volume II THE SHORT GAME AND SCORING and VOLUME III SHORT CUTS TO LOWER SCORES, by Jack Nicklaus With Ken Bowden, illustrated by Jim McQueen. They are published by POCKET BOOKS.

I also read Volume I, THE SWING FROM A-Z, and it is an excellent book, but I got the most out of Volumes II and III.

I cannot recommend these books strongly enough. The information covered is extensive and the tips are presented with illustrated drawings that make the principles easy to understand. These books totally changed the way I perceived the game of golf. They pointed me toward a bridge over the gap in the instruction material I discussed in Chapter 1 INTRODUCTION.

I still read them at the beginning of every season and occasionally during the season. Every time I read them I pick up something new. In these books there are a number of tips relating to full and short game shots along with remedies for specific swing problems. There are also points which had never crossed my mind on weather conditions, mental aspects, trouble shots and course management strategy.

The most important lesson I learned was there is far more to playing this game well than just hitting a golf ball. This point is the basic premise of this book. I then began to analyse every area of the game, emphasizing non-swing aspects, and I believe everything I learned about golf from this point on, evolved from the information in these books.

In the area of course management, the comments in the books greatly enhanced the factors I considered. I was only beginning to understand the issues but I was expanding my knowledge and thinking of more and more factors.

I also began to pay close attention to how the ball was sitting on or in the grass. The term for this is "the lie of the ball". The word lie in golf terminology is used in two contexts. One lie is how the ball is positioned in relation to your feet at address — uphill, downhill or sidehill. The second context is how the ball sits in the grass — bare lie (no grass), fluffy (grass around the ball), down (ball down in long grass) and perfect (ball sitting on top of short fairway length grass).

I studied the way both lie factors affected the trajectory of the shot and the distance it travelled. I learned to make the proper adjustments.

Again from the books I became more aware of the possible affect of wind and temperature on the flight of the shot. This was only the beginning but I at least was aware of these factors and studying them. It takes many seasons to learn the affect these conditions have on an individual's game. I still do not claim to know everything about them.

Jack's books also encouraged me to look at trouble shots as a challenge and not a problem. His suggestions got me thinking and innovating on the course, helping me realize there are many options in recovering from any given situation.

I still had to learn how to choose the proper recovery option but I was at least thinking about the options. Prior to this I would make quick decisions and not think them through. As I was getting into trouble frequently, this had a big impact on my scoring.

In the chapter on STAGE 2, I mentioned that instructional material in magazines and books was often contradictory. I did not find the Nicklaus books contradictory within themselves but I did find some articles which contradicted the information in these books. When this happened I analysed the situation and chose the alternative I felt best suited my game. Again, good books, get them.

During this stage my scores varied dramatically. As long as my best scores are lower than my previous best scores this is a sign of improvement. The better scores show I can play better, it is just that the improvements which allow the better scores have not yet set themselves into my regular game.

This is a common phenomenon for all my stages. There is a large range in my scores, then the range gets smaller, then I move to the next stage. The key being the lowest scores are lower than the previous scores. I wish I had known this from the beginning, I would not have been as frustrated as I was at times.

Early in this stage I decided to keep notes about my game. In the notes I recorded problems I was having and what I was concentrating on when I played well and when I played poorly. In this way I was able to identify recurring problems and tendencies.

I no longer have my original notes because I was always updating them and discarding the old ones. The points are not in any order and are just short phrases to remind me of things to remember and watch for.

The following are my latest edition of these notes:

- Driver. Watch alignment carefully, ball not too far forward, do not reach for ball (stand too far away), proper height of tee, DO NOT START DOWN UNTIL CLUB AT TOP.
- 3 wood. Hands forward, ensure face square, do not swing too hard, allow for tendency to push shot.
- 4 and 5 woods. Keep hands low, do not reach for ball.
- 3 iron. Wait for clubhead at impact (for an explanation see Chapter 10 Subsection 1.5 SHAFTS), do not lift head.
- 4 iron through pitching wedge. Watch ball too far forward in stance, do not lift head, face square.
- Sand wedge around green. Always play ball well back in stance, hands forward.
- Putting. Smooth firm stroke, left elbow out, wrists firm, most break around hole, watch for footprints on soft greens, do not move until stroke finished, head down, pick aiming spot very precisely, allow margin for error to the right (I tend to push putts), watch right hand gripping too tight.
- PATIENCE AND DISCIPLINE.
- Concentration. Keep trying, never give up, keep thinking (note lie, layout, pin placement, etc.), ignore distractions, hit the shots and add them up at the end, do not think of score.
- Hot weather. Swing harder with arms, start with legs.
- Cold weather. Swing easy, watch tempo.
- Stance. Weight back on heels at beginning (I have a tendency to fall forward during the swing).
- Shot selection. Unemotional analysis, do not be stupid, think.
- Confidence. BELIEVE IN MYSELF AND MY ABILITY, decide on club and go, no doubt once chosen.
- Playing well. Smooth tempo, careful alignment, hesitate at top of backswing, slow backswing, thinking way around course well, firm putting stroke.

When I first created this list I reviewed it every two to three weeks and added to it whenever I thought of something. Just reading the list and thinking about the points helped program them into my mind.

During this stage I also expanded the statistics I kept. To the statistics I mentioned in the previous chapter I added the categories of number of

3 putts, number of saved pars, saved bogeys, chip and 1 putt, chip and 2 putts, and chip and 3 putts. All these categories helped identify weaknesses in my short game.

Typical numbers for these statistics were: 3 putts, 3 or 4 per round; saved pars, 1 or 2; saved bogeys, 5 or 6; chip and 1 putt, 2 or 3; chip and 2 putts, 5 or 6; chip and 3 putts, less than 1 per round.

As with the statistics I discussed in the previous stage, just keeping track of these numbers and thinking about the cause of problems immediately after a bad result helped me identify the true cause of the problem.

My first discovery was finding out how bad I was with my chip shots. I then spent a number of practice sessions working on improving my chipping. It took some time but the improvement from these sessions eventually showed up in my game.

My statistics also indicated my long putting was still not very good. I had more than three 3 putts per round. Since I was not hitting a lot of greens in regulation this was too many. Even if I was hitting a lot of greens this would be too many, but with only hitting a few greens this was terrible.

The remedy was to change the target area for long putts. I no longer tried to sink them; I just tried to get them within 3 feet (1 metre) of the hole. I also practiced longer putts to develop the "feel" for knowing how hard to hit a putt to get it near the hole.

At one time I paced off the length of every long putt in order to teach myself the force required for the distance. Once I had the distance I would adjust the number to allow for the slope of the green, uphill or downhill.

Measuring the distance of putts was a useful exercise and I recommend it if you are having trouble getting the feel for the speed of the greens. For me, having a number in my head allows my body to react with the proper force. This will not happen for the first few shots but after awhile my natural tendencies take over. If my last shot was 20 feet (6 metres) and I hit it too hard and this shot is 10 feet (3 metres) I know I must hit the shot with less than half the force.

I also paced off the length of short wedge shots. This had the same benefits as pacing off the length of putts. Over time I became more accurate with them.

During this stage I began to work on controlling my mental thoughts on the course. I started by trying to stop rushing my swing when our group got behind in the flow of play. I exercised the mental discipline to control my mind and not mentally rush my swing when I felt rushed.

I also became interested in the Rules of Golf. I learned the basics and agree that following the rules will save more shots than they cost. Learning the rules completely takes a long time, but a player should at least know the fundamentals and certainly understand the conditions where they are entitled to free relief.

In the second season of this stage I bought another driver. The old driver was just not doing the job and I was convinced a new driver would solve all my problems. In fact the new driver worked well for awhile, but then the old control problems came back again.

When using the new driver I discovered a bandaid remedy for the times when I was spraying my drives in all directions. I found if I lowered the height of the tee and moved the ball back in my stance, I could regain some directional control. The more wildly I was hitting the ball the more I lowered the tee. I paid a penalty in distance, but that was better than being in the trees.

I did have one unusual experience during this stage. I caddied for a touring professional in the Alberta Open, a tournament on the Canadian tour. I enjoyed it but found lugging a golf bag around in hot weather is harder than it looks. After the first day my back was very sore.

The player I was assigned to was from Ontario, Canada. I do not know what he is doing today but I wish him well, he was a very nice guy. He hit the ball like a machine, every shot the same, with a slight draw. I was impressed with his long game.

He did however, have problems with his putting. He hit at least fifteen greens in regulation every round and his best score was 73, and he had a 78 in one round. What was unusual was he did not look like a bad putter, no jerks or anything, the ball just did not go in the hole.

Being a caddie was interesting but I did not learn a lot. I was too busy making sure I did not make any mistakes that might cost the player a penalty. I also did not want to distract him by asking questions. This was his way of making a living and he was serious about it.

After the final round he offered to go the practice tee and give me a free lesson. I declined but thanked him. I declined because I was too embarrassed to show him the golf swing I had at the time.

I remember two incidents from the tournament. The first was in the opening round on the second hole where he asked my opinion on the break of a putt. I gave him my opinion, which was wrong, and he never asked again. The second was he sank a full 7 iron shot from the fairway on a 425 yard (380 metre) hole. It was an excellent shot that bounced once, checked and rolled into the cup. This was the only eagle on a par 4 in the tournament. No putting problems here.

To get my handicap from 13 to 10 I increased my overall level of ability in all aspects of the game. My course management had improved and I was allowing for the lie of the ball and the weather conditions. Most of this improvement was directly attributable to the Jack Nicklaus books mentioned earlier. They gave me the information to get me thinking about factors I had not previously considered.

The other major issues were the statistics and the information about my game they provided, the notes I kept to remind me of recurring problems and beginning to control my mental thoughts on the course.

When I finally got my handicap to 10, I found I could not move down. There was a barrier there which I could not conquer. I seemed unable to mentally accept I was ready to enter the world of a single digit handicap golfer.

I spent a considerable amount of time thinking about my game and came to the conclusion better things were to come and I only had to wait. I was convinced I was a better player than my scores and handicap indicated.

CHAPTER 7
STAGE 4: 10 to 7

Stage 4 lasted three seasons.

When I began this stage I thought I was playing reasonably well. I had played with a number of golfers who had slightly lower handicaps and did not understand why.

The problems they were experiencing were similar to mine and parts of my game were better than parts of their games. They just seemed to take one or two less shots a round. One less drive in the trees, fewer three putts or make one more long putt, or a chip in or whatever. They would just be consistently better.

At first this bothered me and I began to feel frustrated, unlucky and convinced the golf gods hated me. I pouted for awhile.

Then one day I decided to stop sitting around feeling sorry for myself. I obviously had the skill to play better, I was just lacking something. I set out determined to find out what that something was.

I first tried approaching the better players and asking their opinion on how I could drop my handicap. I got the usual answers of they worked harder at their game and I had to work harder on mine. I had to practice more often and hit the ball better and farther.

At that time I was convinced, although I am sure they believed what they were saying, this was not the answer. I was not hitting the ball great but I was hitting the ball reasonably consistently. I was getting the ball near my targets most of the time and all aspects of my game were reasonable. I did have weaknesses but so did they. The answer had to be something else.

I believed these people said these things because most golfers seem to think that to play golf well, one has to practice a lot and hit the ball great. I had seen too many players who did not hit the ball very well at all, but still managed to score better than I did. I was convinced this "beating balls" mentality is a myth.

I agree some practice is beneficial, but I did not believe I had to spend more than an hour or so every two weeks to keep my game tuned. Certainly not hours every day hitting hundreds of balls.

After more discussion with better players and a lot of analysis, I finally came to the conclusion the original advice was partially correct. Yes, I had to work harder on my game, but no I did not have to work on improving how I hit the ball. What I needed was to continue to analyse my statistics, continue to learn and use course management principles,

29

continue to improve my short game and above all continue to believe in my ability.

I told myself I was not trying to learn how to shoot 63, I was just trying to learn how to shoot in the mid 70's. There is a world of difference between these two numbers and I believed I could get to the 75 level with the approach I was taking.

I was further convinced of this by an incident at the driving range. A person was taking a lesson at the stall next to mine. I stopped hitting balls and just listened to what the teacher was telling the player. I did not know either of them, I was just nosy and figured I could get a free lesson.

From the discussion, I discerned the player had a handicap of 14, had been there for years and would do anything to get to a single digit handicap. Near enough to my situation.

At the end of the lesson the teacher told the player that to get to a single digit handicap he would have to hit a lot of good shots. The teacher then went on to tell the player he needed a lot more work at the range before he could even hope to get to that level. The teacher did not mention course management, or the mental aspects, or learning how to play trouble shots or even how to make short putts.

The player listened intently to the teacher and after the teacher left, the player went and bought another large bucket of balls.

As I was leaving I stopped to watch this guy banging balls and actually felt sorry for him. After what the teacher had said he seemed so disheartened. He was trying so hard to hit the ball well.

I went away convinced this fellow had been misled and was wasting his time. I believed he should be spending more time working on the other aspects of his game, like course management, short game, etc.

I do not mean to slander all golf instructors by this story. The professionals I met and talked to at my home course were excellent. I frequently sought their advice and enjoyed talking golf with them.

I may also have been unfair to the teacher. He may have known the students golf game well and have given the best advice for that student at the time. I do not know that.

Nevertheless I remained convinced that beating balls at the driving range for hours was not the magic answer to a single digit handicap. The other aspects I have mentioned are as big, if not a bigger factor. No magic answers, just continue to get better at EVERY aspect of the game.

The issues just discussed relate to my mental attitude. Discovering what I did, resulted in my believing I was taking the proper approach. I now truly believed, in my heart and soul, my scoring would improve.

When I reached this mental state, the mental barrier (to a single digit handicap) was gone and I could get on with learning and playing.

As I mentioned I felt I was a reasonable golfer. I certainly was nowhere near the professional level but I moved the ball around the course all right and could hit most shots with some consistency. I did hit a few bad shots every round but I figured this was just part of the game.

I knew I did not have the time to perfect my swing techniques so I did not have unreasonable expectations. I was hitting 6 to 9 greens per round and my short game was not bad. I could get down in three shots from 100 yards (90 metres) most of the time and sometimes in two. More than three from this distance was rare. The number of 3 putts was still high, around 2 or 3 per round and my total putts were also high at 34 or more.

All in all these were not bad numbers. They were not the numbers for a touring professional who shoots 63, but not bad for someone approaching the level of being able to shoot 75 occasionally.

I was not shooting 75 yet, but I felt I just needed to tighten up a few areas and I would get there. Every aspect of my game was improving and better things were on the way. That is what I thought at the time.

Looking back, I think I was far more optimistic than I should have been. Although I did not realise it at the time I had the wrong equipment, not a great golf swing and really did not hit the ball as well as I thought. Maybe this indicates the power of positive thinking and what believing in yourself can achieve.

Do not get the wrong impression, I was not a bad player, I just was not as good as I thought I was. You do not need to be that good an all-round player to have a single digit handicap. There is hope for almost everyone.

Apart from the progress on the mental side as discussed there were two other major changes I made during this stage. The first was I changed how I hit my driver and the second was I learned how to make short putts.

First, my driver. I was still having problems with this club. My driving statistics revealed I was averaging at least two drives a round in the trees. I concluded I had to improve this, so off to the driving range I went, once or twice a week.

Even though I was convinced beating balls was not the answer, I did justify this short term exercise on the rationale that I was out to correct a specific problem with one club, the driver. I hit a lot of balls with no noticeable improvement in the driving statistics. I was not worried because I knew it takes time for improvements to work into my game, no matter how much practicing I do.

Some time around the fourth week I hit a drive which ended up, of course, in the trees. At this time I was still hitting a high draw off the tee.

After I saw this shot go into the trees I just stood still for a few seconds. I then turned to my playing partners and said simply, "That's it, I give up. Hitting a high draw consistently well off the tee is beyond my ability. I am going back to my fade." And that was that.

From then on, I hit a fade off the tee whenever I can. I can still hit the high draw but I know occasionally one of these is going into the trees. I just accept it. Fortunately there are not too many situations where I am forced to hit a draw.

I knew when I made this decision it was right for me. I realised it was time to accept the weaknesses of my game and not continue banging my head against the wall. I am the only person who knows my game, my skill level and my weaknesses and I am the only one who can take into account all these factors and make the proper decisions.

After I decided to play my natural fade off the tee I tried a number of drivers. The old driver had a closed face and I did not want to use it any more. I finally found one I could hit a consistent fade with.

Changing to a fade off the tee dramatically changed the way I played a hole. Because I became quite consistent hitting this fade I was able to essentially ignore anything left of my target area.

My tee shots would usually go straight or fade up to 25 yards (22 metres). I therefore had a 25 yard (22 metre) target area which I could reasonably expect to hit. When I did miss this area, and this was not often when I was playing well, I would usually miss further to the right.

If there was trouble on the left I aimed down the center of the fairway and would end up in the center or on the right. If there was trouble on the right I just aimed down the left side. I was able to build up my confidence in these shots to such a point where I was actually shocked when the ball went left.

If there was severe trouble on the left, out of bounds for example, I was a little more careful not to hit the shot left. I accomplished this by emphasizing starting my downswing with my legs and swinging easy. Moving my legs first ensured I got my body in front during the swing and for me, resulted in a blocked shot, causing the ball to go to the right.

As a result of my improved driving I re-thought my strategy on every hole based on the premise I would hit a fade to a fairly small target area. I was then able to pick the best spots to approach the greens from and hit that area with increasing frequency. I could actually make use of some of the course management principles I was learning.

I was also able to reduce the number of double bogeys because I was keeping the ball in play. This is the advantage of accurate driving. Distance is good, but past a minimum distance, accuracy is more important. When I kept the ball in play I did not make many double bogeys or higher. Fewer double bogeys is the same as more birdies, they both add up to a better score at the end of the round.

This dramatic improvement with my driving had another effect. As I hit more fairways I had to hit more longer iron shots to the greens. This put more pressure on a different part of my game. As I hit the irons more often my play with them improved. As they improved I began to hit more greens. As I hit more greens I had longer putts. I gradually adapted to these changes and improved in every area.

This is why overall improvements take time to show up in scores. As you improve in one area you put more pressure on another area of your game, which in turn has to be improved. Be patient when you know you are improving but your scores do not yet show it. Accurate driving is worth shots off the handicap, this delay is the reason it does not show up immediately.

The second change which had a big effect was I learned how to make short putts. This is so important to the playing of the game I have devoted a complete chapter to this topic. See Chapter 13, MAKING SHORT PUTTS.

When one cannot make short putts, every other aspect comes under pressure. There is pressure on the long putts and chip shots to get the ball close to the hole. Pretty soon the pressure expands to get the approach shots close. Then to the driver to get the drive in the proper position to get the approach shot close. Every shot eventually becomes a pressure shot.

When I learned how to make short putts this pressure was relieved. I no longer felt compelled to get everything as close as possible, I knew if I just got the ball reasonably close I would get it in the hole. I was able to ease up when playing and concentrate on hitting good shots and the other aspects of the game.

I also did not have to worry about the effect of bad shots because I knew I could save par or make bogey anyways. Remember I was trying to shoot 75 not 63, so a few bogeys are allowed.

Over time my confidence level became so high that there simply was no question in my mind about making any short putt. When I did miss a putt I looked for the real reason the putt was missed. If I could not find an excuse, or knew I had hit the putt very badly, I would accept this as my hitting another bad shot. In no way do I let a few bad shots affect my confidence.

If I reacted to every bad shot (putt or full shot) I would never improve. I would always be trying different techniques to eliminate the bad shots. This is futile. Concentrate on repeating your good shots and the number of bad shots will be reduced.

Of course, if I am repeatedly doing the same thing wrong I would try to eliminate the wrong, but only after I have identified a problem as being persistent.

Due to my improved putting the number of 3 putts dropped to under two per round and my total putts also dropped. I still was not making a lot of putts outside 15 feet (4 metres) but I was making almost all my short putts.

The ability to make short putts accounted directly for almost two shots off my handicap. I am totally convinced of this. At the handicap level of 10 to 7, a one to two shot improvement is a big improvement.

Another factor which helped my game was I began to play from memory. I had played my home course for years and was fairly familiar with it. I tried to remember similar situations in the past and the results I had attained.

This allowed me to adjust to a number of factors which I was not normally aware of. An example is there are some holes that play longer than the distance on the card. I was unable to determine the reason but I allowed for it by taking one more club on the approach.

The biggest gain using memory was on the greens. I certainly cannot remember every putt I have hit but when a putt did something I did not expect, I would note it. At some future time, I would get a similar putt. If I could remember a past putt and how that putt reacted, I had a higher probability of making my current putt.

This is a major point. I frequently hear touring professionals comment on how they remember a previous putt. Many strokes can be saved this way.

During one season in this stage I decided to keep a new category of statistics. These were the scores I made on every hole. After every ten rounds or so I calculated an average. The results surprised me. There were four holes I thought would show a very good average but did not. The holes I was having problems with were the 3rd, 4th, 12th and 16th. A few simple changes in my approach to these holes allowed me to get the averages down to what I felt was reasonable for a player of my ability.

The 3rd is a short downhill par 3 of 144 yards (131 metres). I expected my average to be just slightly over 3.0. The actual average was 3.6, half a shot too high. After thinking about the way I was playing the hole I decided to stop aiming at the pin when it was on the right third of the green. I realised the green slopes sharply away on that side and shots landing there were frequently rolling off the green. Further right was a bunker and when not in the bunker I usually had a tricky chip shot. I was making too many bogeys from this area so I decided to avoid it.

The 4th hole is a downhill par 4 of 293 yards (268 metres) with an array of bunkers in front of the green and out of bounds along the left side. This is an easy par 4 when played correctly and I felt my average was around 4.1. The statistics showed an average of over 4.5. Again another half shot that I felt I could easily save.

My remedy was to simply stop trying to hit the green off the tee. In a number of years playing this hole I had only hit the green once and attempting to do so was costing me shots. I would sometimes go out of bounds or end up in a bunker. I then decided to lay up in front of the bunkers from the tee. I still used my driver but hit it easy.

The 12th hole is a hard par 3 of 216 yards (196 metres). Out of bounds is very close to the left side of the green and definitely in play on the right. My average for this hole was over 4. I expected the average to be more than 3 but certainly not more than 4.

I was making too many double bogeys and higher (too many shots out of bounds) and rarely 3. My original solution was to purposely lay up in front of the green and then chip on. The out of bounds narrows at the green so laying up reduced the number of shots I hit out of bounds.

This did reduce my average slightly but not enough. I was still averaging around 4. Besides I felt like a wimp laying up on a short hole. A "real golfer" would not do so.

After more thought and analysis I realized the real problem was not hitting enough club. I had been hitting long irons or a 5 wood. The hole played directly into the prevailing wind and was slightly uphill. I had instinctively known I did not have enough club so I had been hitting the shots very hard. The result was I hit wild shots and this brought about the high number of double bogeys plus.

I then started to play the hole with a 4 wood and even a 3 wood, depending on the conditions, and not swing too hard. My stroke average dropped to around 3.6. I thought this was acceptable for a player at my level.

I once scored an ace on this hole. A nice smooth easy 3 wood into the cup. When asked which club I used all I said was "The right club". And it was for me.

For the pessimists who like to detract from the accomplishment by asking what a player shot with their hole-in-one, I shot 79 and had to struggle for it. I had a bad front nine.

Back to my stroke averages on holes. The other hole I had a problem with was the 16th, a short par 3 of 138 yards (126 metres). This hole is slightly downhill to a small green with bunkers front and back. If the green is missed there is a possibility of being stymied behind trees or in one of the bunkers. This is not a very hard hole as long as the green is hit. My average here was around 3.6 and I wanted it nearer to 3.0.

My analysis pointed out two problems. One was an uneven tee box and the second was the green was smaller than it appeared from the tee. First my remedy for the tee box. The teeing area is very small and slopes from back to front towards the green. On some portions the slope is significant and in the back corner where the blue tees usually are, the slope is severe. The result was I frequently had a sharp or severe downhill lie.

I was not adjusting to the unusual lie properly and therefore frequently missing the green. I had been hitting a normal 7 iron from the back of the tee box. Off downhill lies I do not transfer my weight fully and therefore I need to hit one more club.

My second problem was not realizing how small the green was. The two front bunkers cut into the green, reducing the effective landing area. I also realised no matter where the pin was, if the ball was on the middle of the green I would not have a long putt. My solution was to just shoot for the middle of the green. Eventually my stroke average came down to 3.0.

Changing the way I played these four holes resulted in a reduction in my average strokes per round. As my average strokes per round went down so did my handicap. I accomplished this with a little thought and common sense. I did not need to spend hours on the practice range beating balls.

In fact practicing would only have made a marginal, if any difference to my scores for these holes. This is the type of issue I was talking about earlier when I mentioned there had to be more to improving my handicap than beating balls at the range.

Another area where I improved was trouble shots. I discuss trouble shots in more detail in Chapter 16 Section TROUBLE SHOTS. The main point I learned was the concept of damage control. Basically this involves thinking through the alternative recovery shots and the possible consequences. Play to save par but more importantly guard against more than bogey. Do not be too conservative but do not take stupid risks where the possible penalties are high.

Also during this stage I began to look at my performance over the complete 18 holes rather than one hole or one shot at a time. In order to drop my handicap further I was forced to do this; there were only so many shots I could shave off.

I began to look for common factors relating to my game throughout the round. This brought up the mental aspects and at this time I focused on improving my concentration. I made an effort to mentally work very hard on every shot. I was not always successful and gave up on a number of bad rounds, but I was beginning to work on improving this side of my game.

There is one story that comes to mind that occurred during this stage. I was at work one day and had a tee time later that afternoon. I was drinking a cup of coffee and thinking about being on the course. Inexplicably, I became convinced I was going to shoot my best game ever that day. I felt really good and felt like playing golf. I could not wait to get to the course.

I left work and drove to the course still convinced I was going to play great. I went through my warm-up routine and still felt great.

Without going through the round hole by hole I did play great. I shot 73 which is 2 over par, and 2 over the course rating.

Still, I was very unhappy with the round. For the first six holes I hit the ball as good as I ever have. I only missed one green and chipped and one putted on this hole for a par. The problem was I took three putts on each of the other five holes.

So here I was, having played six holes, missing only one green and saving par on that hole, and I am five over par. This is a time one is allowed to utter expletives and the like. As I walked from the 6th green to the 7th tee I was thinking about this. I did not get angry. Instead I felt an incredible sense of relief. I knew I was playing above my head and clearly could not take the pressure. The number of three putts was an obvious indication I simply was not mentally ready for a great score. In short I choked.

I relaxed for the remaining 12 holes and managed to make three birdies and par the other holes. A smooth easy 73 (Ha! Choker!). This experience taught me I had potential but was not yet ready for better scores.

In the latter part of this stage I won the first flight of the club championship. This was not the championship flight, but the flight for handicaps 8 to 10. The tournament was two rounds at stroke play.

My handicap was 8 at the time and I shot 78 and 73. I was tied with another player but the committee awarded me the first prize based on a count-back. Still this showed I could play the game at a reasonable level.

Winning this flight convinced me I was a player and boosted my confidence. No I could not shoot 63 but I could shoot around 75 occasionally.

In the last year of this stage, I purchased my Ping™ irons. It took the remainder of the season to become familiar with their playing characteristics. My previous irons were forged and played quite differently.

Overall, during this stage I made big improvements. The main factors which most affected my handicap were my improved driving and learning how to make short putts. Other areas were handling trouble shots, improved concentration, changing the way I played four holes and winning the first flight of the club championship.

There was a definite improvement in my ball striking ability, but not as much as I previously thought would be needed. At the end of this stage I could hit the ball reasonably well. I was fairly short off the tee, 220 to 230 yards (200 to 207 metres) for a better drive, usually shorter, and consistently hit fairways. I hit my fairway woods well, my long irons not too good, middle irons okay, and short irons well. My short game was not too bad and my short putting was excellent.

I was still learning how to think my way around the course but improving there. I tried to keep the ball in play at all times and score no worse than bogey on any hole. I was looking at the game of golf as a game requiring a sequence of shots not just one shot at a time.

My mental attitude was excellent, I had never been more confident. Any doubts I had about my approach to improving had been erased. I was convinced I was channelling my energy into the right areas and the only direction I could go was down (handicap wise that is). With my new Ping irons I was ready to conquer this game.

CHAPTER 8
STAGE 5: 7 to 5

It took me years to accumulate the total information I discuss in this book, but a fair amount was collected during this final stage. In my discussion of this stage I only touch on the highlights and major issues. The remainder of this book covers the extent of my knowledge in all these areas and I believe is the appropriate knowledge for a person to learn how to shoot 75, occasionally.

Stage 5 lasted slightly longer than two seasons. Generally, the lowering of my handicap in this stage was due to improvement in every single aspect of my game. And I do mean every single aspect, from hitting the ball better and more accurately, to my knowledge of adjusting for lies and weather conditions, to my understanding of course management principles, to my damage control, to my short game and to my handling of the mental aspects. I can honestly say I improved most areas of my game at least 100 percent.

When I began this stage I was very enthusiastic about my prospects. I thought about golf all the time. I read everything I could find on the game. I spent hours analysing my statistics and thinking about how I should play each hole of my home course. I set golf at a very high priority in my life and excluded a number of social occasions in order to play. In short I did everything possible to put in place all the conditions for me to play my best. I was consumed by the game and loved it.

Initially, when my scores did not reflect my optimism I did become somewhat frustrated. I then remembered the lesson I had learned where I must be patient and accept the fact improvements take time to show up in my scores. I was patient to a point of exasperation. I kept telling myself my approach had brought me this far and I was convinced it would continue to work for me. I had faith in my game and faith in myself.

I could understand the delay in achieving better scores early in this stage as I was still getting used to playing with my new Ping irons. But after I learned how to use these clubs I was at a loss to explain why the very real improvement in shotmaking was not showing up in my scores.

When comparing the old forged irons to my new heel-toe weighted clubs, I felt the performance difference was significant. Mediocre shots I hit with the Pings ended up on the green where the same shot with my old irons would have been short. This helped not only my performance on the course but also increased my confidence. This should have resulted in lower scores.

Looking back, I would say it was just a matter of letting the scores come down naturally. Perhaps I was trying too hard and pushing my game to limits it was not yet ready for. When I eased up and relaxed my scores came down.

I was so impressed with the performance of the Ping irons I bought a set of Ping woods. I quickly discarded the driver, because I hit big slices with it, but I kept using the fairway woods. I was very happy with their performance. With the exception of the driver (and putter) I will not play any other brand of club.

I was convinced I had finally found the correct equipment for me. I will try other clubs but they must work spectacularly well before I will integrate them into my existing set. It took me many years to find the correct clubs and reach this level of confidence with them.

During this stage I continued recording the statistics I mentioned in the previous stages. When reviewing them I found I was still having trouble with three holes on my home course, the 4th, 7th and the 17th. The changes I made illustrate my improved course management knowledge.

The 4th is a downhill par 4 of 293 yards (264 metres). I had changed the way I play this hole during the previous stage but I felt the average was still too high for a player of my perceived ability. This is an easy par 4 and I felt my average should be very close to 4.0. The statistics showed the average was over 4.2. I should be able to save almost a quarter of a shot per round.

My remedy was to stop hitting my driver off the tee and to use my 4 wood instead. With the driver the ball was occasionally ending up in a group of trees on the right. Using my 4 wood left me short of the trees and if blocked, far enough back to shoot over the trees. This simple change brought my stroke average down near 4.0.

The 7th is a very difficult uphill par 3 of 235 yards (214 metres). There is a bunker about 5 yards (4 metres) short of the green and the terrain slopes towards this bunker. A shot landing short of the green and not on the far right of the fairway will usually roll into the front bunker. From here, it is difficult to get close to the pin because of the distance from the green. A long bunker shot is a hard shot.

I wanted my average on this hole to be under 4.0 and my statistics indicated the average was more than 4.3. In the past I had been hitting my driver trying to get the ball on the green. My solution was to use my 3 wood off the tee. I would aim at the right side of the fairway and could normally hit the narrow landing area. If I hit the shot perfect or if the ground was firm the ball would roll onto the green. If I did not hit the shot perfect it would usually stop just in front of the green and I would have a chip shot. As long as I hit the small landing area the ball would stay out of the front bunker. This change dropped my average for this hole to under 4.0.

The third hole requiring a change in my tactics was the 17th. This is a dogleg left par 4 of 415 yards (374 metres). To the left is out of bounds and trees for the total length of the hole. This was a hard hole for me and I expected my stroke average to be around 4.4. My statistics showed an average very near 5.0. Not good.

Big hitters can cut the corner of the dogleg. I am not a big hitter. If I hit a perfect drive (swung at hard) on the correct line I can cut the corner. The problem is although I hit many good shots I do not hit every shot perfectly. In the past I had been trying to cut the corner and more often than not the ball was catching the trees as it was coming down. The result was the ball either deflected out of bounds or stayed in the trees.

I decided to stop cutting the corner and hit a 4 or 3 wood, depending on the conditions, down the middle of the fairway to a point past the beginning of the dogleg. This left me with a clear shot, but a longer one to the green. If the wind is strong and assisting, I still try to cut the dogleg but only then. This changed dropped my stroke average to around 4.4.

Again, here are more examples of how to save shots by thinking about strengths and weaknesses. These changes had a direct affect on my handicap dropping.

I must point out that even though my stroke average for holes was dropping, the amount of strokes saved did not directly translate into strokes off my handicap. This is partly due to the effects of averaging and partly due to the handicapping system. Not all rounds are counted for handicap purposes. In the long run of course, my improvements did help to reduce my handicap.

All through this stage my shotmaking improved. I became more accurate with my driver, hit my new Ping fairway woods well and even learned to hit my long irons reasonably well. My short game also continued to get better. I became more aggressive with my wedge shots and when I had a chip shot I tried to sink it. I even became a little more bold with my long putts, although I was careful when I may have a tricky second putt.

The key to the improvement in my short game was the ability I discussed in the previous stage, the ability to make short putts. I could afford to be aggressive with the short game shots because I knew how to get the ball in the hole. One of my opponents once commented that I could get up and down out of a ball washer. Not true, one is entitled to free relief from a ball washer.

During this stage I also worked on my mental attitude. Once a person learns to hit the ball reasonably well the mental aspects become more important. These are discussed in detail in Chapter 11 MENTAL ASPECTS. The topics covered are Confidence, Concentration (and Choking), Discipline and Temperament.

I improved in all these areas. In the area of confidence I convinced myself I was a reasonable player and had a reasonable level of skill. I was not as good as a touring professional but on some days I could actually come close to playing the game in the manner in which it was meant to be played. When I had a problem I either accepted it as a bad day or if it was a recurring problem, I knew I would eventually fix it. I trained myself to never doubt my ability.

With concentration, I worked very hard on disciplining my mind to focus on the game both between shots and during the shot. I formalized a number of detailed routines and checklists which helped me keep my mind on the shot and all the various factors I had to consider when planning the shot.

In the area of discipline, I made every effort to ensure my ideal golfing environment was in place. I set up a strict personal regimen and stayed within this regimen. This included time management, frequency of playing and physical conditioning.

With my temperament I learned to diffuse my emotions before I played my next shot. I toned down my emotional outbursts and generally improved my behaviour on the course. I accepted bad breaks and bad shots because I had come to the realization they were just part of the game. Well, most of the time.

The detailed routines and checklists mentioned are described in Chapter 15. During this stage I formalised them and reviewed them regularly. They include routines for the pre-round warmup along with full shots and putts. I also developed practice routines and home drills which I performed regularly (every two weeks). These were a definite factor in my improving.

Another area addressed during this stage was on course problem diagnosis. I had been keeping notes and noticed the same small group of problems kept creeping into my game. Because I was aware of the possible problems I could recognise the symptoms while on the course and immediately take corrective action. I also developed drills to correct some of these problems and reduce the likelihood of them recurring.

On course diagnosis is a result of my getting to know myself, my skills and my game. This takes time. The same applies to the remedies for each problem. The final remedies I ended up with are based on a number of experiments, some of which worked and many which did not. Over time I learned what were the correct remedies for each problem. I discuss these in Chapter 14 PROBLEM DIAGNOSIS.

I also learned the rules. I attended a three day seminar on the Rules of Golf put on by the Royal Canadian Golf Association. A heavy seminar, very tiring. On the last day we wrote an exam. I was one of the few who passed the exam out of a very large class. In fact, I got the highest mark in the class.

Passing this exam was a great boon for me. I had again been questioning my approach to the game because my handicap still was not low enough. The results of the exam showed I at least had some intelligence and there was a chance my approach was correct. I felt if I could learn the rules as well as most people then I could analyse my game and the game in general as well as most. This was a great boost to my personal confidence, not only in golf but in all areas of my life.

I did have one unusual problem during this stage which had my playing partners questioning my sanity. The course had recently installed a watering system and I thought they were putting too much water on some of the tees.

Occasionally, I could feel myself sinking into the ground when I made my swing. The feeling resembled being on a ship which is rocking. This caused no end of problems with my driver. I was unconsciously compensating for the sinking by lifting my upper body as I came through the ball. When I make compensations like this the ball can go anywhere. Once I figured out the cause, I knew this was going to happen, or at least expected it and was careful not to swing hard.

I asked a number of other players if this had occurred to them and most just looked at me as if I was crazy. Others thought I was trying to use gamesmanship on them. I was not; I was serious. I watched some of the other players hit on holes where this happened and some did slip. I could not tell if they sank, but their right foot did noticeably move during their swing. To this day I am convinced I was sinking.

The point of this story is I did not immediately react to the bad shots I hit due to this sinking. I had become so confident in my ability that when things did go wrong I did not automatically assume the problem was my fault. Instead, I analysed the situation and determined the real cause of the problem.

43

I did complain to the Board of Directors of the club about over-watering, but no one listened to me. Although a couple of weeks later I noticed the tees seemed to be a bit drier.

During this stage I recorded my scores and calculated my handicap every few rounds, more often if I was close to a breakthrough. Consequently I knew what scores were needed to drop my handicap to the next level.

This was true when I was nearing the point for a 5 handicap. I had been playing very well for the past few weeks and knew my handicap was approaching my magic number. I was playing one round where I reached the 17th tee needing to play the last two holes in one over par or less.

On the tee I decided to play conservatively. I hit a smooth easy 3 wood to the middle of the fairway and this put the ball 190 yards (171 metres) from the middle of the green. The pin was at the very back so I had about 200 yards (180 metres) to the pin.

I hit a smooth 5 wood that landed near the middle of the green and rolled just off the back stopping on the fringe. This left me with a 15 foot (4 metre) chip shot. I sank the chip for a birdie. I actually hit the chip a bit fat, but it still went in. I guess it was just meant to be.

Under the handicap rules (Equitable Stroke Control) the maximum I could take on any hole for handicap purposes was double bogey. Therefore no matter what I did on the 18th hole I was guaranteed to get the 5 handicap. When I sank my chip I knew I was now a 5 handicap. I lost control of myself and yelled out loud "I made it!". I was excited to say the least.

For the pessimists who always ask "What did you shoot on the 18th hole?" the answer is my birdie putt lipped out, and I made a par. For the other pessimists, my score for the round was 74.

As an indication of my scores, following are sample handicap differentials during this stage:

15	15	13	9	6	9	13	12	3	14	6	13
8	8	5	8	9	8	7	9	8	6	7	7
9	5	4	10	6	6	9	12	13	12	9	16
8	9	7	12	9	12	8	11	6	8	13	10
4	9	7	9	7	10	10	3	13	4	9	8
7	8	7	5	6	8	4	5	9	12	6	10
9	5	4	5	0	7	8					

The handicap differential is the difference between the score and the course rating. At Highlands, where almost all these rounds were played, the course rating was 71. There is an occasional 75 (or better) there.

I have deleted the early season scores because they were played on temporary greens (which are temporary holes cut in the fairway). I have also removed scores from the end of the season because they are too high and I do not want to be reminded of them.

After all these positive issues I have discussed, there is one negative point I must bring up. I had one problem with my game that I was unable to solve. About a month before I got to the 5 handicap I got the dreaded yips. Yes, believe it or not I had the yips when I got my handicap to 5.

My version of the yips seems to be a little different than the common version. The common version seems to affect people with their short putts. With my version, the problem was in the 20 to 40 foot (6 to 12 metre) range. Putts shorter or longer were not affected. The problem did not cost a lot of shots but it did cost a few.

What happened was my right hand would take over (jerk) during the forward part of the putting stroke and hit the ball an inconsistent distance and direction. I tried a number of technique changes but could only fix the problem for a short time before it returned.

I do not consider my version of the yips debilitating. The reason I say this is I think, the key word here is "think", I know why I developed my version of the yips.

I believe my yips are the result of a combination of two factors. The first is I was actually choking under the pressure of playing well. When the yips started I was playing better than I had ever played. I had a chance to make some very good scores and knew it. At the time I was convinced if I was going to shoot very low rounds I had to start sinking a few putts from these problem distances. I had started to really try to make these putts. Conclusion: I choked.

The second factor was the condition of the greens. The speed of every green seemed to be different. I asked the course superintendent about this and he said there were some differences in speed but not a lot. He then made what I consider to be a very significant comment. He said he was overseeding the greens to change the type of grass.

Well, I had been playing on greens with different types of grasses and did not know it. The new grass was growing well on some greens and on others it was patchy. No wonder I had been having trouble getting the speed right.

I believe the inconsistent green surfaces created doubt in my mind as to the proper speed for a putt. My uncertainty contributed to my right hand coming into the stroke. While I was making the stroke I was frequently not sure I was hitting the ball hard enough. Consequently my hand would, at the last second, try to hit the ball harder. This was a subconscious reaction.

I came away from this grass issue learning three things. The first was to be a better player I had to learn the types of grass available and how to identify and read the speed of each. I still do not know how to do that.

The second was I obviously was a very good short putter to have my handicap drop under these playing conditions. The third was to make an effort to be informed about what is being done to the golf course. Changes like this affect the playability of a course and cost uninformed people needless frustration and heartache.

So for me to rid myself of the yips all I need to do is what I have been saying all along, I have to believe in my ability. If I do this I am sure the yips will disappear. This problem is no different than any other I have faced and it can be solved with the same approach, analysis of a situation to find the true case of the problem and determine the proper remedy. Enough negative vibes, back to the positive.

I finished this stage with a handicap of 5. I saw this as the reaching a goal after a very long and difficult struggle. I was thrilled beyond words.

Looking back, I consider the overall improvement to every area of my game as the major contributing factor in attaining the skill level I achieved. The equipment I used helped, as did changing the way I played a number of holes at my home course. These had a direct affect on my average score per round and therefore my handicap.

The refining of my on course problem diagnosis and the appropriate remedies allowed me to make corrections to my game during a round. This had its biggest impact when I was playing poorly. It allowed me to turn a number of poor rounds into mediocre rounds and occasionally save a good round. The net effect was a reduction in the total number of shots I averaged per round.

Learning the rules was another factor. Knowing the rules can save shots. Attending the rules seminar and passing the exam also boosted my confidence.

Another two factors that contributed were the improvement in my mental attitude and the formalizing of my routines and checklists. I made dramatic advances in all aspects of the mental side but especially in confidence and concentration. Golf at this level is very much a mental game and these improvements definitely made me a better player.

The formalizing of the routines helped ensure I did not forget to consider the myriad of factors required to get the ball to a target area. By regularly reviewing and refining them I was able to reduce the number of mental errors I made during a round. Consistency and the reduction of errors are important. The routines helped by creating a consistent approach to every shot and reduced the chance of a small error occurring.

At the end of this stage I was at least twice as good a player as I was at the beginning. I had improved every aspect of my game so dramatically I was surprised my handicap was not lower. I was very disappointed when the season ended because I felt there was still room to drop my handicap.

Then I remembered how hard this game really is. And the effort I had made to get to this point.

Instead of feeling disappointment I think I will sit back and enjoy the feeling of accomplishment I deserve.

These are the stages I went through in learning to shoot 75, occasionally. Now I have reached this level I can play with anyone. When I mention my handicap golfers accept this as a reasonable level of skill and consider me A PLAYER.

The remaining chapters of this book explain the issues and factors I have discussed in more detail. I hope they are as useful to you as they were to me. I would like everyone to have the ability to shoot 75 occasionally. Perhaps then we could love to love this game instead of hate to love it.

75 Occasionally

CHAPTER 9
CHOOSING A HOME COURSE

In this chapter I discuss the issues to consider when choosing a home course. By home course I mean the course you will join as a member or the course you will play most frequently.

If you presently have a home course and are happy with it, this chapter will be beneficial in helping you see the strengths and weaknesses of your course. If you do not have a regular course or are considering changing, this chapter will help you select one that will allow you to play your best.

Choosing a proper home course is important because this is where your handicap will be maintained and it is where you will have the best chance of shooting your lowest scores. The major issues are:

1. KNOW THE STRENGTHS OF YOUR GAME AND CHOOSE A COURSE THAT ALLOWS YOU TO PLAY TO THOSE STRENGTHS. To be able to play your best golf, your home course must suit the strengths of your game. The alternative is to change your strengths so they suit the course, which is what most people attempt to do. Some succeed and others do not.

The issues to consider here are:

1.1 STYLE OF PLAY. The overall style of your game. To illustrate, look at two types of golfers. Golfer A hits the ball very long but frequently offline. His wedge game is acceptable but his real strength is his long iron play. He is also a very good putter from 30 or more feet (10 metres). Golfer B is a short hitter but accurate. His short game is excellent but his long irons are weak.

Golfer A will do better on a long course that is fairly wide open and the rough is not too penal. He will also score better on courses with larger greens. Golfer B will play better on a short course where there are few long par 4 and par 3 holes. The difficulty of the rough and narrowness of the fairways will make little difference to him.

1.2 LENGTH OF COURSE. This is major. I hope this is changing, but at my home course anyone who even thinks they are something of a golfer always plays from the back tees. Part of this seems to be macho and part of it the desire for people to compare their game to that of the touring professionals. A good score from the back tees means you are that much closer to the professionals.

For the handicap player this may not be realistic. To give an extreme example there are courses where the tee shots require a 230 yard (210 metre) carry over rough. Many handicap players cannot hit the ball in the air that far. I cannot. In this situation playing from the back tees is a exercise in frustration.

The length of the course also relates to the clubs you will be using. Will you be required, again based on your own game, to hit a lot of long irons and fairway woods. If these are your strength or you play them reasonably well then this is fine. If you cannot hit a long iron but are good with fairway woods you may need to change your set make up.

Also remember once you join a course you will find yourself using certain clubs more than others. As you continue to play and use these same clubs you will improve your skill with them. There is a natural tendency to have the strengths of your game be based on the course you play. Make allowances for this. However joining a course where you have to play a large number of 2 irons into elevated greens will not necessarily make you a good 2 iron player, and probably won't.

1.3 FIRM OR SOFT GREENS. If the greens are hard and you are forced to play shots that land short of the green and run on, your scores will probably be higher. If you must land 30 yards (metres) in front and the ball has to bounce and run the remaining distance you have limited control on where the ball finishes. If it happens to land on a downslope the ball may run too far. If it lands on an upslope it may not run as far as you want or may even stop dead. It may also land in a wet spot and stop quickly or a side slope and kick way offline. Essentially this type of shot requires you to read the prospective path of the ball from the middle of the fairway.

I believe this introduces too high a luck element into the shot and does not allow the player with the skill to hit the ball the correct distance to get the consistent result he deserves.

Consistent results mean better scores. If you have correctly figured out the shot needed for the situation and hit a good shot, you should get the results. I have heard touring professionals complaining about courses where if a shot was 1 or 2 feet (30 to 70 centimetres) off from the optimum position, the result was dramatically different. For a chip shot this degree of accuracy can be achieved. However, from 180 yards (165 metres) out, even the best players in the world cannot be that precise.

For handicap players such issues have a bigger effect on their game. If a shot takes a bad bounce and ends up off the green, the professional has a higher probability of getting the next shot close to the pin due to his higher level of skill. The handicap golfer has a lower probability of getting the next shot close. Over time these probabilities add up to shots lost and a higher handicap.

On courses where the greens hold a reasonably well hit shot you will have a better chance of scoring well. If you are able to hit the ball the correct distance and with the proper trajectory to hold the green, you have a higher probability of a good result and a larger margin for error. When you can fly the ball into the green you do not have the case where if you hit the ball 2 feet (70 centimetres) shorter you may stop dead and be 20 or 30 yards (metres) from the green which can happen in a run up game.

There are hazards here also in that the green may have big swales and the ball may be knocked away, or there may be firm and soft spots. The difference is the end result. On a green that holds a reasonable shot you will usually stay on the green even if you get a bad bounce. With the run up shot you could end up a long way away from the green itself. Again, back to probabilities.

When I use the phrase "greens hold" I do not mean every shot no matter how poorly hit, will stop dead. I do mean a shot hit reasonably well will stop within a short distance. For example a high wedge shot with a lot of backspin should stop within 10 feet (3 metres) most of the time. A 3 iron, again hit high and reasonably well should stop within 30 to 40 feet (10 to 12 metres). The shorter the stopping distances the better.

1.4 PUTTABILITY OF GREENS. I would not want to play a course where all the greens are perfectly flat, this would be boring. However there is the other extreme best exemplified by mentioning Augusta National and Royal Melbourne. Both these courses are known for their treacherous greens.

Having not played either of these courses I am not sure if they are only made difficult for the professional tournaments. Even if this is so I would not want to play these courses regularly. I admit it; I am not a good enough putter to handle extremely tricky greens.

I also know I never will be a good enough putter because I am not willing to spend the time required to learn how to play greens such as this. Leave it to the guys playing for hundreds of thousands of dollars. I do not need the aggravation. Some professionals have commented they do not need the aggravation either. In short I prefer to play a course with greens of moderate difficulty.

Related to this point is how the ball rolls on the green. If the greens are rough and the ball is frequently deflected your score will be higher. To shoot low scores the greens must be in good shape. At the lower handicap level how the ball rolls can dramatically affect not only your score but your concentration. If putts hit well are being deflected it is difficult to keep trying to make them.

1.5 DIFFICULTY. Are there water hazards, fairway bunkers or out of bounds in your playing area. Is the rough exceptionally penal and the terrain hilly. Are there a lot of greenside bunkers, elevated greens, blind shots. These all increase the difficulty of a course.

If the greens superintendent regularly sets the tees in difficult positions and tucks the pins the course will play harder.

1.6 WATERING SYSTEM. Regularly watered courses are usually in better condition than a course without a watering system. They tend to play longer because the fairways are softer and the greens usually hold better. The rough may be thicker and require more strength to play out of.

1.7 WHETHER YOU PREDOMINANTLY DRAW OR FADE THE BALL. Most courses favor one type of shot. For example Augusta National is said by some professionals to favor a player who hits the ball right to left (draw, or fade for lefties). This does not mean every hole favors a draw, there are some that favor a fade, but more holes play easier with a draw. To determine the bias you should look at the following factors:

- Are there a number of holes where the tee shot must draw or fade to get to the proper landing area. This can be due to the placement of bunkers and water hazards.
- Are there a number of dogleg holes that go in the same direction.
- Do a number of fairways slope in the same direction.
- Do trees or bushes surrounding tee boxes and greens force a draw or a fade.
- Is there out of bounds, frequently on the same side.
- Is the best approach position to a number of greens consistently on the same side.
- Do a number of greens slope in one direction making it hard to stop the ball unless you hit into the slope.

To visually determine some of these factors can be difficult. My suggestion is, like Ben Hogan is reported to have done, to walk the course backwards, starting at the 18th green and ending at the 1st tee. While making the tour look where the optimum position seems to be for each shot and where the approach to this position would come from. From this "reverse angle", the course can look quite different.

Another possibility is to hire a helicopter and fly over each hole as Jack Nicklaus has done.

1.8 LIGHT ROUGH. Some courses cut all their fairways at the same height, others cut a landing area at normal fairway height and the remaining grass slightly higher. This is known as light rough or contoured fairway. Having light rough beside the fairway landing area can be an advantage as long as it is not too thick or too high. The light rough will sometimes stop an errant shot from going into the trees or other trouble. When all the grass is at normal fairway height the ball will roll more.

A disadvantage is the light rough will cut down on the distance of your drives if your ball lands or rolls into the longer grass. If the landing areas are too small or cut incorrectly, this can end up costing a significant amount in lost distance.

The second disadvantage of the light rough is it is more difficult to control the ball out of the longer grass. You can get flyers (shots with little spin on them) due to the grass getting between your clubface and the ball.

I think the advantages outweigh the disadvantages. I prefer the light rough to be there.

2.   PICK A COURSE WHICH ALLOWS YOU TO HAVE THE LOWEST HANDICAP. All that is involved here is looking at the course rating and Slope. Your handicap is based on these numbers. If you pick a course on which you will score well allowing for the strengths of your game and has the highest course rating, you will have the lowest possible handicap.

Be realistic in your assessment. The rating is based on length and difficulty and as the number gets higher, the harder it is to score on the course.

3.   PUBLIC OR PRIVATE COURSE. An interesting question. I believe if you are serious about improving your game you should at least consider a private or a semi-private course.

Personally I make every effort to avoid playing on public courses. I freely admit to being a golfing snob but it is more involved than that. Although there are some reasonably good public courses I find the following can and do occur frequently on public courses:

- The course is not manicured. The greens and fairways are shaggy.
- Bunkers are not raked, divots not replaced, areas of the course damaged, etc.
- The greens are as hard as concrete.
- The flow of play is very slow. Although there are many who play a lot on public courses there are a few who do not. This minority can slow up every group behind them.
- You may be forced to accept a stranger into your group who may not know even the basics of etiquette.

If you play a public course you simply have to be prepared for these and not let them affect your game. Of course there are some excellent public courses. I am speaking generally and suggest you check out all the factors outlined here before you make your decision.

You may find similar situations on a private course as well, but they are less likely to occur because people have spent what is usually a significant amount of money to join. Therefore they have a real stake in all aspects of the course and are more prone to be concerned about, and conscious of issues such as I have mentioned.

4.　COST. The total annual cost of playing and any other expenses. This includes initiation fees, green fees, assessments, meals and drinks, other facilities if applicable (pool, tennis courts, etc.) and the cost of driving to and from the course.

You may also want to consider the cost of items in the pro shop. I believe the club professional should be supported and I buy my clubs and accessories from him. I do expect to pay slightly more for things like golf balls than at a discount store but I accept this as being part of the cost of the service. Every club professional I have met has been interested in the problems of my golf game. At times they have provided a sympathetic shoulder to cry on and a place to seek advice. Any small extra cost is worth it.

I can also say I have always been treated fairly in all my dealings with the pro shop at my home course. I have never felt I have been overcharged or taken advantage of.

5.　LOCATION. What is the travel time to the course from your home and work. Also consider weather factors. Seaside courses frequently have more wind than inland courses. Some areas get more rain and some may be colder. Is there noise from adjacent areas, for example an airport next door.

6.　PEOPLE TO PLAY WITH REGULARLY. For many this is the single overriding factor in choosing a home course. They tend to join one where friends or acquaintances are already playing. Or as in my case, they know someone who can get them in as a member.

When I first joined a regular group I was just happy to have someone to play with. It did however work out very well. We all had common interests and surprisingly, we all tended to improve at a similar rate.

What I consider to be my perfect golfing group would have the following characteristics:

- Our personalities do not clash and we get along well. Having one or two people who tell a lot of jokes is good.
- We are serious golfers out to play golf and enjoy the game.

- We are interested in the game and willing to spend time talking golf. This includes having enough interest to read the golf magazines, some books and follow the professional tour. In other words we keep up with the developments and happenings in all aspects of the game.
- We are all reasonably good players. This includes from handicap 18 down. Ideally I would like everyone in the group to be better than I was, as long as they give me shots with our bets.
- Everyone knows golf etiquette.
- They hit the ball reasonably straight. By this I mean they are not always hitting their ball into the bush. I do not mind looking for balls occasionally but if it becomes too frequent it bothers me.
- They want to play the same number of times per week, and at the same time. I like to play four times a week and it can be difficult finding people who play this often. I also prefer to play after work on weekdays and on the weekend between 8:00 A.M. and 10:00 A.M. Playing before 8:00 A.M. is not pleasant for me. I do not like to get up too early and it always seems to take a couple of hours before I wake up no matter what time I get up.

A side note here is some groups can be very closed when it comes to letting new people into their existing group. Accept this, it happens in all walks of life. A good idea is to try to find a large group of more than eight people because it may be easier to infiltrate. Or try looking for twosomes and threesomes.

The make-up of the group can also affect performance. Some like to be the best player in the group so they can act as a mentor. Others like to be the high handicapper so they are always under pressure to stay with the others.

You get to know the people you play golf with very well. There is something about the common battleground you go through that seems to bring people together.

7.   TIME TO PLAY. If the usual time for a round is more than 4 hours, your personal time may be stretched too tight or you may become frustrated at the pace of play and let it affect your concentration.

8.   HOW BUSY IS THE COURSE. Can you get the tee times you want. If you cannot get on the course when you have the available time, you end up not playing as often as you should.

I also want to be able to book tee times with a minimum of hassle. I know people who stand in line at 4 A.M. to get a weekend time. I refuse to do this. I also like to be able to get a tee time at least two days in advance so I can plan my personal schedule. I hate wasting hours standing around the first tee waiting to get on the course.

Another concern here is the number of outside tournaments the course allows. If they are too frequent they can affect your access to the course.

9. MAINTENANCE. To me, an extremely important issue. The condition of the course dramatically affects my ability to play well. The grass must be cut regularly, bunkers raked and the course kept in tip-top shape. This allows me to make the shots I have spent years gaining the skill and knowledge to execute.

Also look at how the ball sits on the grass on the fairways. If the grass is not thick the ball will sit down on the ground (not the grass) and this will increase the difficulty of the course.

10. GENERAL MEMBERSHIP. Do you want to make business contacts, social contacts or both. Are the members generally of the socio-economic group you want. If you decide to bring a guest who is a business associate or client are you worried who may want to join your group.

11. GOLF TOURNAMENTS. Does the course have a regular number of social tournaments. My club has a Mens League handicap tournament every second Thursday and a number of club tournaments during the season. These are excellent for meeting other members.

12. JUNIOR PROGRAM. Is there a program for juniors. I have seen kids spend a lot of time hitting golf balls at the course. There are a lot of worse places they could be.

As you can see there are a number of issues to be considered when choosing a home course. Not all are equally important to everyone. If you choose the right course, you at least give yourself the opportunity to have the factors in place to play your best and have the lowest handicap.

It may not be possible to find the perfect course but knowing what the drawbacks are and making a decision to accept them can reduce or even eliminate any frustration you may feel.

CHAPTER 10
EQUIPMENT

Can a person buy a better golf game? The answer is yes, to a point. There is no doubt certain equipment will help a player save shots. There are real differences in the performance characteristics of different brands of the same generic equipment. The key is to know the differences and choose the types that best suit your individual game.

My comments on specific types or brand names of equipment is how I found them to work for me. It is important to note another player may find the performance characteristics of the same equipment to be quite different. This could be due to any of the myriad of factors involved, such as swing speed, swing angle, purity of contact, strength, and so on.

I believe my study of the different performance characteristics has helped me understand the strengths and weaknesses of my own game to a fuller extent. This knowledge has been a factor in my becoming a better player.

In the following sections I make a number of comments on how various clubs perform when I mishit a shot. To some this may seem a negative position. I do not see it that way. I believe accepting I am going to mishit a number of shots, and in fact a high percentage of shots, is simply accepting reality.

By choosing equipment which performs well when I do hit bad shots, well not too bad, is just taking advantage of available technology and providing me with the opportunity to play the best I can. A shot saved is a shot gained.

SECTION 10.1 — CLUBS

The clubs I use regularly include:

- Northwestern DF driver with metal head and steel "kick" shaft.
- Yamaha X-200 driver with graphite head and shaft.
- Ping 3, 4 and 5 woods.
- Ping irons 3 through sand wedge.
- Ram Zebra mallet putter, weight adjustable, one of my two favourites.
- Ping Karsten model blade putter, the other of my favourites.

When choosing a club I must like the look and feel of the club. I cannot explain what it is that appeals to me, I just have to like the look of the club. The club must also feel right in my hands, especially when I waggle it. I like a club with some head weight, although this varies on the club. With the driver I like to feel the head of the club as I swing it, with irons and putters this is not as important.

SUBSECTION 10.1.1 — WOODS

There are three categories of woods; the driver, fairway woods and trouble woods. In the points following I discuss the issues I consider when evaluating woods.

When choosing a driver, I prefer one with a high swing weight (heavy head). Swing weight is a measurement of the weight of the head of the club compared to the total weight of the club. A club with a heavy head will have a high swing weight and a club with a light head will have a low swing weight. This measurement is different than the overall weight of the club, which may also be heavy or light.

I prefer the heavy head because when I swing the driver the momentum of the clubhead will help keep the driver on the path I have started. Or in other words, it takes an effort from me to pull the driver off the original path of the swing. My metal driver has a D5 swingweight, which is high. My other clubs are C9 which is slightly lower than average. Average being D0 and D1.

Metalwoods have proven their worth. The performance characteristics vary depending upon the brand but every metalwood I have tried puts less spin on the ball. The advantage is the ball will fly straighter because less sidespin is imparted and therefore hooks and slices will be reduced.

The disadvantages are because of reduced backspin the ball will not fly as high and if you want to turn the ball intentionally it is more difficult. The lower trajectory can be remedied by using a high trajectory ball or by using a metalwood with more loft or more weight in the lower part of the clubhead. The increased difficulty of curving the ball intentionally can be remedied by practice with the club.

One problem I have experienced with a number of wooden drivers is the amount of bulge and roll they have. Bulge is the amount of curvature vertically on the face of the club and roll is the amount of curvature horizontally. Bulge and roll are normally good things because they help correct a mishit shot. If the ball is hit off the toe for example, the roll will cause some draw sidespin to be imparted to the ball. The result is the ball will not end up as far offline.

The problem is the amount of bulge and roll on the drivers I have tried was too severe. This had the effect of creating a too severe draw trajectory, at times even a hook. I do not like this because a prefer a shot to go straight, or right of the target and not have the possibility of going left.

This is another reason I like the metal driver. If I hit a shot off the toe the ball goes straight even though there is a loss of distance. I prefer the slight loss of distance to the chance of the ball going left. I can then stand on the tee and know I am not going to hit the ball left unless I hit a bad shot. This is a tremendous advantage when I have to drive to tight fairways or there is trouble on the left.

Another factor to look at when choosing woods is the face angle at address. Some woods are manufactured with a closed face, others square and some with slightly open faces. This can be corrected at address by simply turning the clubface, but I do not like to hit clubs with a normally closed face.

I am deathly afraid of hitting a snap hook and just seeing the closed face is enough for me to make adjustments to my swing. This can cause all sorts of problems which can be very hard to diagnose. I prefer a club with a square or slightly open face.

I also want my driver to perform well with different swing speeds. I may want to swing hard because I need extra distance or I am angry. Or I may want to swing easy and place the ball in a specific position.

The shaft on the metal driver broke a few games ago (during a normal shot) and I have been using the graphite driver. The performance characteristics of the graphite head are similar to those of the metal head.

Now on to the fairway woods. First the 3 wood. I see my 3 wood as having three purposes. The first is a highly accurate club with reasonable distance from the tee, the second is a distance club with some accuracy off the fairway and the third is for trouble shots to keep the ball very low, for example under tree branches, and still get as much distance as possible.

I also look for a 3 wood which performs reasonably well with a shot hit thin (very low on the clubface). With shots off very short grass I tend to hit the ball thin and such a shot should get some height, fly straight and go a fair distance.

What I really need in a 3 wood is a club that when I hit the ball high on the clubface (off a tee) the ball will fly high and straight, and when I hit the ball low on the clubface (off the fairway) the ball will get some height, be fairly accurate and provide as much distance as possible.

Now the 4 wood and 5 wood. I use these clubs off the tee for height to clear obstructions and off the fairway for height and distance. I also want a reasonable level of accuracy with all shots. I like to hit fairway woods and find them much easier to play than long irons. Being a relatively short hitter I use these clubs frequently on longer par 4's. The woods I presently use perform well in the above situations.

I have thought of changing to metal fairway woods from my Ping fairway woods but the main reason I have not done so is I cannot find a set that has the same swing feel as my irons. I do not have the skill to adjust my swing for too many different clubs. I can handle a different driver because I swing it differently, but I cannot handle the difference with other clubs because I like to swing them roughly all the same.

Besides, I have two holes-in-one with my 3 wood, how could I get rid of it?

Trouble woods or as some people call them utility woods, are useful clubs. I carried one some time ago and found it excellent for getting out of light and medium rough. If you play a long course with contoured fairways you should consider getting one. I stopped carrying my trouble wood when I cracked the head after hitting a shot off the heel. I have since been unable to find another brand that has the same swing feel as my other clubs.

SUBSECTION 10.1.2 — IRONS

I own two complete sets of irons. One is a high quality forged set (blade -not peripheral weighted) and the other is investment cast (Ping Eye). Each type of club has its advantages and disadvantages. My comments on the differences in irons are based on my personal experience with one specific brand of each type.

The benefits of forged clubs is they impart more backspin on the ball and it is easier to curve the ball. When hit very well these clubs provide a more consistent result than the investment cast clubs by a small margin. The key here is "when hit very well".

The disadvantage of the forged clubs I have used is their small sweet spot and unforgiving character. If hit anywhere other than the sweet spot a heavy penalty is paid.

The sweet spot is the optimum position on the clubface where the ball should be hit. It can be located by holding a club in the air with two fingers and using a ball to tap the clubface. When the club does not twist when tapped you have found the sweet spot.

The Pings have a larger sweet spot and are more forgiving on mishits. These clubs also impart less back and side spin so the ball will fly straighter.

The disadvantages of the investment cast clubs are the ball will not stop as quickly on the green and it is harder to intentionally curve the ball. The fade or draw can still be achieved, it just requires a more exaggerated action to get the desired result. The stopping power on the green can be increased by using a ball that accepts more spin.

For me the advantages of the investment cast clubs far outweigh their disadvantages and any advantages of the blade forged clubs. I am a convert. The performance on mishits is enough to convert me. I know I have hit shots with the Pings that ended up on the green when a similar shot with my forged clubs would not have.

One problem I have heard discussed with investment cast clubs is the quality control. Of course there will be poor quality cast clubs on the market just as there are poor quality forged clubs. If you do decide to buy a set be careful which brand you choose and check them prior to purchasing them, if at all possible.

A few simple checks will help you verify that there are no major problems. Start by asking the club professional to weigh all the clubs (if he has a scale). All clubs should have the same overall weight. The second test is to check the swing weights are the same. For the above two tests the sand wedge may be heavier. The third test is to line the clubs along the wall with their soles as flat as possible on the floor. Visually check the shafts get gradually longer, the lie of the club changes and the lofts decrease.

These checks will not ensure you will get a perfect set but they will at least increase the probability of your not getting a totally mismatched set. I special-ordered my Ping irons, so I was not able to do the checks before receiving the clubs. I was not worried anyways, I knew Ping has an excellent reputation for quality control. I have since done the checks and all is well.

Be aware minor flaws can be easily corrected, so if a problem is found listen to the suggestions of the professional.

Before you purchase a set of clubs talk to the club professional. Every pro I have talked to knows a lot about the differences between brands of clubs. I also suggest you talk to people who play the brand you are considering and ask their opinion.

Ideally, the best test is to play with the clubs before making your decision. I was convinced to buy the Ping irons after a fellow I worked with let me use his for a weekend. I thought was a very nice gesture and was extremely careful to take good care of them. I did not try any stupid shots that might have damaged them and even went to the point of checking the area around the ball for loose stones that could scar the club. Before I returned them I cleaned them.

If anyone is interested, the specifications for my Pings are Red lie, standard length, standard grips. I like the idea where I get custom-fitted clubs. I feel I am slightly different than the average person, a little shorter and average build.

Another factor to consider when looking at clubs is the lie. The sole should be flat on the ground when you take your address position and more importantly, when you hit the ball. If the toe is in the air the club is too upright. If the heel is raised the club is too flat.

There is a way to check the lie but it is not a recommended procedure. You can hit balls off a colored rubber mat and then look at the bottom of the club. If the colored marks are at the toe or the heel of the club the lie may be wrong for you. If you want to do this with a demonstration club the professional may get upset, and justifiably so. Doing this also voids any manufacturers warranty I have ever seen. When I do this I am careful to swing easy.

I prefer a sole which is slightly rounded from heel to toe, has a sharp leading edge at the bottom of the clubface and has some but not a lot of bounce (with the exception of the sand wedge).

I want the sole to be rounded because if I am standing a little more upright or flatter than usual, due to temperature, tiredness, etc., the effect on the shot will be minimal. A sharp leading edge will help the club cut through longer grass and the minimum bounce is so the club can be used off tight (bare) lies without hooding the clubface.

As with the woods, a big issue is how the irons perform with a shot hit thin. I hit a lot of shots thin and want the club to give me a good result.

One thing to be aware of is many sets of irons have a distance gap. With my forged set I could hit my 9 iron only a few yards (metres) further than my wedge. The 9 iron had exactly the same length of shaft and was only a few degrees stronger in loft. This created a big gap between my 8 and 9 irons.

I have also seen a case with cast clubs where a fellow had a distance gap between his 9 iron and pitching wedge of 25 yards (22 metres). This guy was a very good striker of the ball and I personally saw him hit a number of shots with both clubs. The gap was there for him.

Some sets of irons have a small difference in loft between the long irons which can result in a player hitting two clubs almost the same distance. This is more prevalent among those who are not strong swingers. There is only a marginal difference between a 2 iron and a 3 iron in distance for me. Therefore I do not carry a 2 iron.

Distance gaps and minimal distance differences can be corrected by changing the loft of the club, installing a longer shaft and increasing the weight of the clubhead with lead tape (see Subsection 1.6 LEAD TAPE). Talk to the club professional about these things, they can help.

When I changed from forged to investment cast clubs a number of adjustments were required. It took almost a whole season for me to fully adjust my game to the new irons.

The biggest adjustment was due to the hosel offset. After some experimenting I ended up moving the ball back almost an inch (2.5 centimetres) in my stance. This sounds obvious now, but it was not at the time.

The next adjustment was in the alignment of the clubface. The new clubs appeared to be aimed left of the target at address which resulted in a tendency to open the face as I brought the club through the impact area. The remedy was to go through my clubface alignment drill (see Chapter 15 Section 5 DRILLS) until I trained myself to accept the alignment as proper. It took a few weeks before I was totally comfortable with the alignment.

I also had to change the clubs I used for chip shots. With the forged clubs I chipped with my 7 and 8 irons depending on the distance required and where I wanted the ball to land. With the cast clubs I found the 7 and 8 irons performed differently. The type of ball used here is a factor but there still was a big difference.

With the Ping 7 and 8 irons the ball tended to come off the clubface "hot" or very fast. I found it extremely difficult to control the distance of a short chip shot. After trying other clubs in the set I concluded the ball came off the sand wedge the slowest, the pitching wedge was a little hotter and the 9 iron a little hotter again.

The end result is for very short chips and touch flip wedge shots I now use the sand wedge. For longer chip shots of 20 to 40 feet (6 to 12 metres) I use my 9 iron and beyond this the 8 iron. I may use the pitching wedge in the 20 to 40 foot (6 to 12 metre) range depending on where I want the ball to land. The point I am making is that I had to learn to chip with different clubs.

Another adjustment was with the sand wedge. Performance characteristics of sand wedges vary dramatically and there were big differences between my new sand wedge and my old one. I had to learn how to use the new one. This took some time and required a number of practice sessions in bunkers.

I am convinced the Ping sand wedge is a better club than my old one. The Ping sand wedge performs well with a normal explosion shot, however due to the design of the Ping wedge (and this is totally dependent on the specific brand) I can handle buried lies in bunkers with some degree of accuracy.

No, I cannot put a lot of backspin on the ball and stop it immediately out of a buried lie but I can get a consistent result based on the force of the swing. When I say buried lie I mean a "fried egg" lie or where the ball is buried a little more.

With my Ping sand wedge I close the face to a point of almost zero loft and hit down right behind the ball. As the club goes through the sand I can feel the club lifting to pick out the ball. Over time I learned to judge how far the ball would run, depending on the force applied.

This is a shot I did not have with my previous sand wedge. With my old set, if I had a buried lie I would take my pitching wedge and try to dig the ball out with hand action through the ball.

Although the Ping sand wedge performs very well in deep sand the bounce of the sole is not so large to require a major adjustment when chipping. Even on tight lies I do not have to move the ball far back in my stance in order to negate the bounce. A very good and versatile club that meets all my requirements.

The last adjustment I made with the Ping irons I learned as a tip from a golfer about to embark on the U.S. mini-tour. A mutual acquaintance at the club arranged a game with him. A very fine all round player and a nice guy, I wish him well.

He also used Pings. On one hole he had a severe sidehill lie with the ball well below his feet. I was on the other side of the fairway and did not see him line the shot up. He was about 100 yards (90 metres) from the green and as I looked up, he hit a shot which landed about 10 feet (3 metres) from the pin.

I had been having no end of problems with iron shots below my feet and when I got to the green I asked him how he played the shot. Very casually he explained that because the iron was offset, these types of shots had to be played way back in the stance, with the face hooded. In severe cases the ball had to be so far back as to be outside the right (rear) foot. If the ball was played further forward, the hosel would contact the ground before the clubface got to the ball. When this happened the clubface would be slammed shut and a poor shot would result.

He also pointed out an unknowledgeable player would think he had hit the shot fat and would incorrectly diagnose the cause. I had been thinking I hit the shots fat just as he had said. I had learned something, an advantage of playing golf with better players.

I mention these adjustments to point out that when a player changes clubs there may be differences in the performance characteristics. If you are having problems with new clubs do not immediately assume these problems are due to your lack of skill, give yourself time to adjust.

Overall I am very pleased with my Ping irons. I am absolutely convinced they helped me reduce my handicap. The peripheral weighting does provide the performance benefits.

SUBSECTION 10.1.3 — PUTTERS

Choosing a putter is an individual thing. What works for one person may not work for someone else. With me, as with other clubs I need to like the look and feel of the putter. If it passes this test I try it. I take it to the practice putting green and hit a few putts with it.

On the putting green I check to see how I naturally line up to the target line with the putter. If I tend to aim right or left with this particular putter I decide whether this can be remedied easily. This decision comes from experience, I now know whether I will have an alignment problem with a specific putter.

I also check the size of the sweet spot. I want a putter with as large a sweet spot as possible. The larger it is the more consistent results I will get on slightly mishit putts. With a putter that has a small sweet spot, a putt hit off the toe will go right of the target and not roll as far. With a larger sweet spot the amount the putt is offline and the distance penalty is reduced. This can make the difference between making a short putt and missing it. On long putts this can result in being closer to the hole after the first putt, which in the long run means you will make more of the second putts.

Using a putter with a small sweet spot can also affect your confidence in judging the speed of a green. You may hit one putt on the sweet spot and the ball rolls further than you expect. You hit your next putt softer and slightly mishit the putt and it goes much shorter than you expect.

In this example, you may be hitting the putts with the proper force, but the reason you are not getting a consistent result is due to your inconsistency in hitting the sweet spot. This can lead to what one of my golfing buddies used to call "windshield wiper putting", one putt long the next short, and so on.

The two putters I use, the Ping Karsten blade and the Ram Zebra mallet both have fairly large sweet spots. They are forgiving putters and give good results with mishit shots. I have used both these putters for years and have concluded the Ram Zebra is a little better for long putts. I find a long putt mishit off the toe of the Zebra rolls a little better with a little less distance penalty than a shot hit with the Ping. The difference is not dramatic, but it can make the difference of perhaps a couple of feet (half a metre) and this may be the difference between making or missing my next putt.

The other advantage the Zebra has over the Ping putter is the base of the Zebra can be removed and from zero to three washers installed or taken out to change the weight. When playing fast greens I take the weights out and with slower greens I put some or all of the weights in. This way I do not have to adjust the force of the stroke as much. I like this feature. With the Ping putter I can add or remove lead tape to accomplish the same thing, but adding lead tape just does not have the same pizazz.

The Ram Zebra came in a choice of three lies; flat, medium and upright. I have a medium lie but should probably have a flat lie. I tend to hold my hands low and bend over quite a bit when I putt. If the lie of your putter is not correct ask your club professional to bend it.

If you are the type of person who taps their putter on the ground or against their shoe, check the loft and face angle every so often. It does not take much to knock a putter offline. Club professionals who fix such problems should charge a good price in order to help "punish" the player for hitting the bad shots which resulted in him damaging his equipment.

I interchange my two putters whenever I feel like it. There is no particular reason for me to change. There are times I prefer a blade putter and times I prefer a mallet putter.

SUBSECTION 10.1.4 — GRIPS

Another factor to consider is the grips. No one can play well if they cannot hold onto the club. When my grips are slippery I tend to clamp onto the club tightly and this can ruin my swing.

I prefer the rubber composition grips because they work well in all weather conditions. I once had a club with a leather grip but found the leather got slippery in very cold weather. Some rubber grips are too rough for my hands and give me blisters.

After trying a number of different brands I now use Ping grips on my Ping clubs, a TACKI-MAC grip on my driver, a Master grip on my Ping putter and a Tiger Shark grip on my Zebra.

I have medium large hands but prefer a small grip on my driver. The smaller grip makes it easier to get my hands more into the shot, and for me this means a few extra yards (metres). I know a number of people who prefer their driver to have a built-up grip. They say this gives them more distance. To each their own. I use normal sized grips for all my fairway woods and irons.

For me the grip on the putter is important. It has to feel comfortable and sit well in my hands. I prefer a grip with a flat spot on the front, for comfort as well as alignment. The flat spot helps my alignment by providing a consistent reference point to grip the club. If I grip the club in the same position every time I have a higher probability of aligning the face properly.

During the season I clean the grips at least once every two weeks. It is surprising how dirty they can get. This cleaning increases the tackiness and the life of the grips. I am amazed at how many people neglect their grips. Slippery grips cost shots.

I think this so important I will explain the process. To clean the grips, first turn the tap on and adjust the water to a temperature that is very warm but not steaming hot. For each club:

- Wet the grip by running water over the complete grip.
- Sprinkle a cleansing powder like Comet or Bon Ami™ on the wet grip. Two or three short shakes of the tin is usually enough unless the grip is very dirty.
- Take a stiff brush and scrub all of the grip. The brush I use is fairly stiff but not as stiff as a wire brush.
- Scrub the grips hard while turning the club. Do not worry about using too much force, the grips are sturdy. The cleaning powder should lather around the whole grip. If there is not enough lather add more powder and continue scrubbing.
- Rinse the grip thoroughly.
- Dry the grips with a towel.
- Lay the clubs across a chair or against a wall. Do not put them back in the bag until they are completely dry.

I replace my grips after two seasons whether they need it or not.

I once got cheap and did not replace the grips on my 3 and 4 irons because they did not seem to be worn. After a month I replaced them also because I was able to notice the difference in the feel of the thickness between the new grips and the old grips. I did not like having this different feel on my clubs.

When playing be sure to keep the grips as dry as possible. A shot hit with a club slipping or turning in your hands may go anywhere. If it is raining and your towels get wet, rub the grips under your arms on your shirt or on the inside of your trousers. These areas normally stay dry in the rain. This is only a last resort. Be aware rubbing the grips on your clothes may leave marks which are very difficult to clean. I have ruined a couple of shirts doing this. Of course, this is a small price to pay for a good golf shot.

The grips are a major part of the golf club and must be considered when choosing a club. If you like a club but not the grip, get the grip replaced.

SUBSECTION 10.1.5 — SHAFTS

It has been said by many knowledgeable people that the shaft is the most important part of the golf club. To be honest, I do not know a lot about the shafts available on the market today.

All I do know is the shafts I have on my current clubs work reasonably well for me. If you would like an explanation of the performance characteristics of the different shafts discuss them with your club professional.

All my irons have standard Ping shafts which I believe is stiff. I do not know or care about the shafts of the putters. My driver has a Northwestern kick shaft and I am not sure if it is stiff or not, the label has worn off.

The reason I stopped using my Ping driver was I suspect, due to the shaft. I hit big, and I do mean big slices with this driver. When I swing this club I have the distinct impression the clubhead is lagging behind the shaft at impact.

If I was a strong swinger I could understand this, but I am not. I thought perhaps there was something wrong with the club itself but I have asked regular players of Ping drivers to try my club and they all claim it is fine. I have also used their drivers and I slice with their drivers.

I have this same feeling of the clubhead lagging behind with my 3 iron, although not as pronounced as with the Ping driver. To compensate, I change the tempo of my swing with the 3 iron.

As I write this I am thinking how I alter my tempo. I have just realised I decelerate my hands and arms through the impact area. Decelerating through the impact area is not good. Maybe this is why I sometimes have problems hitting this club crisp and frequently hit it shorter than I feel I should.

I have this problem only with the Ping driver and 3 iron. If it was the shaft that comes with the set I would have the same problem with the fairway woods too, but I do not. I hit them with my normal tempo and usually hit them very well, without the feeling of waiting for the clubhead to catch up.

I guess it is time to find someone who can tell me if the problem is due to the shaft or if it is an inherent flaw in my swing. Interesting, I will have to look into this.

I have had an extra long boron/graphite shaft installed on my Ping driver. The shaft is 4 inches (10 centimetres) longer than normal. I decided to try this shaft after hitting a golfing buddy's driver equipped with one of these shafts. I hit the ball much farther with his club.

My club worked well for a few rounds but then suddenly I could no longer control it. I have gone back to my old driver but will try this club again when I feel my swing is in the right shape.

I mentioned earlier I was not concerned about the shafts on my putters. I have tried a few of the extra long putters and am concerned about the shaft with them. Of the four brands of putters I looked at, all the shafts seemed to be too flexible for my liking.

This probably would not matter on a short putt but I wonder about a long putt. When a long stroke is used I suspect the shaft may bend slightly and kick the putter head through at impact. If this is so, the timing of the stroke for a long putt becomes critical. If the timing is off, the shaft may kick the head earlier or later than the impact point, causing an inconsistent force to be applied to the ball.

When I tried one of these putters on the practice green I was unable to prove my theory but I did get the feeling of the putter head lagging behind my hands. Perhaps it was just the brand of putter. Obviously the pro's who use the long shafted putters either do not have this problem or know how to control it.

When looking at shafts the proper length is also important. If the clubs are too long or too short, you will have to build in compensations in your swing. Your club professional can help you determine the proper length.

SUBSECTION 10.1.6 — LEAD TAPE

Lead tape is available in strips about an inch and a half (4 centimetres) long and half an inch (1 centimetre) wide. As the name suggests these strips are made of lead. They have a sticky side and can be attached to clubheads. One strip of lead tape adds approximately one half a swing weight to the club.

I use lead tape for two purposes. The first is to make the club heavier and the second is to change the weight distribution of the clubhead in order to correct a swing problem or an undesirable performance characteristic.

With my driver and the putter I use lead tape to make the club heavier. On the driver I use the tape to increase the weight of the head with the aim of achieving more distance and a higher trajectory. I attach the tape at the back of the clubhead, as low as possible. With the tape too high, the extra weight would move the center of gravity of the club higher, resulting in lower shots. With the tape as low as possible without being on the sole, I hope to change the trajectory to a higher one.

As mentioned earlier, with the putter I sometimes use lead tape to adjust for different green speeds. For a slow green I add lead tape and for a fast green I remove tape. This takes some experimenting in order to judge how much to add or remove but over time you learn what is correct.

Lead tape can also be helpful with a distance gap between clubs. By adding tape to the shorter club you make it heavier and may be able to hit the ball further, therefore reducing your gap. With my forged irons I put lead tape on the 9 iron because there was a large distance gap between it and the 8 iron. The tape did reduce the gap by about 5 yards (4 metres).

The second purpose, changing the weight distribution of the clubhead is useful when I am having a problem getting the clubface square at impact. This is occasionally a problem for me, occurring with one or two clubs at a time.

For example, if I am continuously hitting my 3 iron with an open face I put lead tape at the back of the iron near the hosel. This makes the toe of the club lighter and theoretically easier to bring to square at impact. If I am drawing with a club I put the tape on the toe. This theoretically makes it harder to close the clubface at impact. Using lead tape in this manner seems to help. I have no scientific proof that it works and it may be all psychological, but I have noticed an improvement.

When I am trying out a new club I use lead tape to fine tune the performance characteristics. I am then able to determine if a club works well with my swing. Many people spend hours practicing with a club in order to change their swing with the club. I prefer to change the club to suit my swing, not change my swing to suit the club.

If you decide to try lead tape start with one strip. You can add more later after you have tested the effect of the first strip. The most tape I have ever put on a club is three strips. I want to be careful not to add so much weight that the flex characteristics of the shaft are changed. Added weight means more stress on the shaft during the swing. Too much tape may also change the balance of the club making it harder to control.

By the way, do not add or remove the tape during a round. Doing so is considered changing the playing characteristics of a club and is against the rules. Once you start the round you are stuck with the weighting for the whole round.

SECTION 10.2 — BALLS

When choosing a golf ball, the factors to consider are:

1. THE WAY THE BALL REACTS TO CHIP SHOTS. I want a ball which is not "too hot" when hit softly with my sand wedge. By too hot I mean the ball comes off the clubface very fast when hit with a soft stroke. The slower the ball, the more I can control the chip shot and the greater my margin for error. These characteristics should not vary significantly in different temperatures. Some balls get "hotter" as the temperature gets colder.
2. DISTANCE OFF THE TEE. I want as much distance as possible without sacrificing the other characteristics.
3. SPIN. The ball must accept a reasonable amount of spin. The ball must stop quickly on the greens and hook or slice with partial (three-quarter swing) shots. I occasionally need to intentionally curve the ball with trouble shots.
4. TRAJECTORY. I want a trajectory which is not too low because my natural tendency is to hit the ball low.
5. WIND. The ball should hold the line well with a strong crosswind and not balloon (rise quickly) into a headwind.
6. DURABILITY. The ball must not cut or scar too easily and last a few rounds without the paint wearing off.
7. PUTTING. I prefer a ball which again is not "too hot" but also does not require too hard a swing to hit it 60 feet (18 metres).
8. FEEL. I cannot describe this "feel" but I just have to like the way the ball feels when hit with my clubs, both full shots and short game shots.

I have played with balls that felt soft and mushy and others that felt rock hard. I prefer something in the middle. This feel must also be reasonably consistent in all temperatures.

For me, the most important factor is how the ball reacts with the short game shots, including putting. I will not use the ball I hit furthest from the tee because it is too hot around the greens.

Distance is the second most important factor. I need reasonable distance to score, but not at the price of playability around the green. I do not have to hit the ball 300 yards (270 metres) but I do want to be able to hit it more than 210 yards (190 metres).

The third most important factor is how well the ball holds the line in the wind. These are the three most important factors. The others are secondary but I still consider them.

I have recently tried the Precept EV balls. Like the previous Precept balls I used for years they seem to have a softer cover that accepts spin and are not too hot with the short shots. I get good distance with them also. I will probably continue to use them until the manufacturer makes a change that I do not like.

I have found balls which perform exceptionally well under certain conditions and have tried changing ball types based on the conditions (wind, for example). I stopped this because I find the other playing characteristics are too different and I am unable to adjust to the differences easily.

For example, there can be big differences in the force required to hit a ball specific distances on the greens. Two balls can be hit with what I feel is the same force, and one will go 20 percent further. My inability to adjust to this difference negates any improvement in the other categories I may have gained by switching balls.

I question the quality control of cheaper balls. I stopped buying them long ago because I got inconsistent distances with them. Not from a flyer lie but just an extra 15 yards (metres) or so every so often when hit well. If you play a ball where this occurs, do not question your skill. First look at the other factors such as the grass around the ball and the weather conditions. If it is not due to these, then change the brand of ball you use.

In short, do not play with "hacker" balls. They can cost you shots by creating doubt in your ability. I only buy balls from the pro shop at my home course.

Even with the top line balls I watch for inconsistency. If a ball does not seem right I get rid of it. I do not find a bad ball often, but it happens.

Most manufacturers produce a range of balls with performance characteristics designed for different types of players. Ads in the golf magazines usually explain what each specific ball is designed for. I suggest reading the ads to see what each ball promises in performance and if the promises appear to be what you are looking for, try the ball. Use it over a number of rounds in different weather conditions to see how it performs based on the way you hit the ball. Also consult your club professional, they know a lot about the differences in performance.

SECTION 10.3 — GLOVES

Whether a golfer chooses to use a glove or not is a matter of individual choice. I prefer to use a glove for all shots. I like the feel the glove gives me on the club and the extra measure of firmness it seems to give to my hand.

The two most important issues when choosing a glove are the fit and the grip on the club. The glove should be fairly tight but not so tight as to cut off the circulation. The fingers should be the proper length with no overhanging material. Watch for stitches that irritate your hand.

The second issue is the grip the glove provides on the club. I select the glove I am going to use based on the weather. If it is warm or hot I use a leather glove because the leather breathes a bit and gives me the best feel of the club.

In cool and cold weather I use a glove made out of polyurethane. This glove is marketed as a wet weather glove. I use it in the rain also, but I find it superior to leather in cool and cold weather. It does not get as stiff and gives me a better feel. In the rain it also does not get as slippery as a leather glove.

Check your gloves for signs of unusual wear. My gloves occasionally wear on the palm where the end of the grip sits. This indicates I am letting go of the club at the top and re-gripping. If you find unusual wear and you are not sure of the cause consult your golf professional.

SECTION 10.4 — SHOES

Golf shoes do two things. They provide a firm base for the golf swing and support for walking. A firm base is essential. If a person is slipping and sliding around, there is no hope of controlling where the ball will go.

I have always used spiked golf shoes. I like the thought of having something digging into the ground to provide support during a shot. I also like the sound the spikes make when walking on asphalt. Hearing this sound makes me feel like a golfer.

I have played with a fellow who wore spikeless shoes and he thought they provided good traction at all times and were even better than spikes in the wet. They may be worth trying.

When choosing a golf shoe an important factor is the fit. I have had several pairs that felt great when I tried them on in the shop but after a few rounds bothered me. My feet would be sore and uncomfortable by the 12th hole. I am convinced the pain distracted me and cost me shots.

The only solution I found is to keep trying different brands of shoes until you find a pair you can wear regularly. Once you find a comfortable pair, stick with that brand.

The shoes must be strong enough to support the forces generated by the golf swing. Even for an amateur these forces can be considerable. The material must not stretch to a point where your feet will slide around inside the shoe. This can undermine your confidence and affect your timing during the swing.

When I was in Australia I was watching a well known pro play in the Australian Masters and noticed that his feet seemed to be moving inside his shoes during his swing. I suspect that this was due to his shoes having stretched from normal wear and this may have affected his balance. He was having problems hitting his driver straight at the time and perhaps the shoes were the cause.

When buying shoes, allow for the fact your feet can swell. I usually try to buy my shoes on a hot day because this is when my feet are swollen. On cool days to counter the difference in my foot size, I wear heavier socks.

Shoes can have a bigger effect on one's golf game than most people realize. It is essential to the playing of the game to have shoes that are comfortable and provide a firm base during your swing.

SECTION 10.5 — CLOTHING

The purpose of clothing is to provide protection from the elements, cover certain body parts and for some, to present a fashion show. Clothing is a part of equipment, especially in inclement weather.

For me, the clothing I wear on the golf course is dictated by the weather. I dress for the conditions. Because how I dress is so dependent on the weather, I discuss the specific aspects within Chapter 12 WEATHER FACTORS.

Generally I dress to look like a golfer. A golfing buddy once made the comment "If I cannot be a golfer, I can at least look like a golfer." I do not try to be a fashion leader but I do wear moderately trendy clothes.

I like to wear golf shirts with the name of a golf course on them. My home course name is okay, but the name of a prestigious course or one a far distance away is better. My personality quirk.

I buy practical and comfortable clothes. I do not spend a lot of money on them, in fact I am cheap.

SECTION 10.6 — GOLF BAG

When buying a golf bag my first consideration is the size. I like a bag large enough to hold my fourteen clubs plus a few extra I may decide to carry. I want to be able to pull a club out of the bag without the grips becoming tangled or rubbing together.

The bag must be sturdy in the areas which receive a lot of wear, such as the umbrella holder, zippers and the places where it will rest on a pull cart. The bag should not be too heavy and have section dividers in the club storage area. It should also have a number of clips for hanging bag tags and towels on and have matching head covers.

I am very fussy about the colors of my bag. I have to like the look of it and am convinced the colors can affect my psychological attitude while I am playing. A bright red bag makes me a little more aggressive. My present bag is bright red with black borders.

Above all, the bag must look like the bag of a golfer. The bag must also have a lot of pockets. I store quite a few things in my bag and want to be able to get everything into it and have easy access. I try to keep everything I could possibly need during a round in, or on my bag.

SECTION 10.7 — GLASSES

For those of us who wear glasses, they are part of our equipment. They help us to see better.

When wearing glasses I find I have two problems, one major and one minor. The major problem is the distortion the lenses can cause when viewing a target. The minor problem is when playing in the rain the water can accumulate on the lenses causing a distraction and further distortion.

The distortion due to the curvature of the lenses is not significant in normal every day life, but in golf, where a person needs to be very precise in choosing a target area, it can be a problem. If you look directly through the center of the lens there is no distortion. As your line of sight moves to the edge of the lens the curvature will distort what you see, causing an object to appear to be in a different position.

For me in golf, the distortion is a factor in two areas, alignment and short putts. With alignment, I have developed an elaborate routine to ensure I choose a proper mark on the ground to line up to. A very minute error here can make a large difference in where my ball will finish. This routine is described in Chapter 15 Section FULL SHOT ROUTINE.

With short putts, the hole as I see it out of the corner of my eye is not where it appears to be. I have to be very careful I do not putt to this false hole position. I accomplish this by concentrating on putting over a spot on the ground in front of the ball. I also make sure when I am addressing the putt and take a quick look at the hole, I turn my head and do not just move my eyes. By turning my head I can keep my eyes in the center of the lenses and can see where the hole really is.

Until I figured this distortion factor out and corrected for it, I lost a lot of shots. I was hitting full shots wide of my target and continually putting to the false hole on the greens. These lost shots were not due to any lack of skill on my part but due to a quirk of my equipment. As I have said before, when you have a problem do not immediately assume it is a reflection of your ability to hit a golf ball. Look for the real reason.

The second problem with glasses is the rain. In the rain I always wear a visor to keep the moisture off the lenses. When the wind is blowing and the water is getting under the visor I wipe my glasses prior to almost every shot. This at least keeps the amount of streaking to a minimum.

About twice every season I apply an anti-fogging solution to the lenses.

When wearing glasses you must also consider the color of the tint in the lenses (if your glasses are tinted). The tint can affect the clarity with which you see the rolls and breaks on the greens and is dependent upon the available light conditions. A green tint will sharpen your view on bright days and a yellow tint will help on cloudy days.

I was once given an incorrect prescription. The lenses corrected for astigmatism in both eyes when I only required it for one. I played golf for a month with these lenses and played very badly.

I finally went back to get them checked and when the doctor apologized for the error I laughed and told him I had lost a lot of money on the golf course because of this. He apologized again and obviously felt bad. I told him not to worry about it, I had not lost any more money than usual.

I once had a lens fall out of the frame on the second hole. I was unable to get it to stay in the frame and had to play the remaining holes without my glasses. Of course I played badly and lost the match. I now carry a special screwdriver for my glasses in my bag.

CHAPTER 11
MENTAL ASPECTS

It has been said that golf is sixty, eighty or ninety percent mental. The number depends on who is making the statement and in what context. The fact is, the mental side of golf is significant.

The mental aspects can be more important than the mechanics of the swing, the correct alignment and aiming procedure and a smooth putting stroke all added together. You need these things to play well but once you have learned them, without the mental side of the game being in a correct state you will not score well.

The mental side includes confidence, concentration, discipline, temperament and gamesmanship. These are all very complex issues and subject to normal human emotions and weaknesses. Conquering and learning to control all these aspects will allow you to obtain the correct mental disposition to perform at your best. This is not an easy task. Below I discuss these aspects and how I handle them (most of the time).

SECTION 11.1 — CONFIDENCE

The better a player gets, the more important confidence becomes.

Simply stated you must have confidence in your golf game. You must truly believe that despite whatever realities the golf course will throw at you, you have the ability to play well.

It is natural to have times when you doubt your ability. Everyone goes through this, even the professionals. As long as you believe you are a good player even when you are playing poorly, you can still turn things around. Never give up, always try your best.

When I have talked to a number of higher handicap players about their game in detail, they invariably say they are only out to enjoy themselves and are not really trying too hard. Although the words sound valid I believe this is only a way of showing their lack of confidence.

With further questioning, most indicate they have had some good rounds and have hit a number of good shots. They do however seem to view these as flukes and not the norm.

I believe they should look at the good rounds and shots and realise they have the capability to play well more often. Not necessarily all the time but certainly far more frequently. They need to accent the positive and accept the negative.

This basic doubt many high handicappers have must change before any improvement can be made. To quote from a famous speech by JFK

"Some men see things as they are and ask why, I see things as they might be and ask why not?"

When I am playing regularly I am confident I can play well. Should I have problems during a round my first reaction is to watch for a pattern in my shots. Once I determine a pattern exists, I begin thinking about the cause and possible remedies. In my case, a recurring set of problems creep into my game regularly like clockwork. Knowing this is a result of the mental analysis of hundreds of rounds and requires some, but not a lot of effort. I discuss my recurring problems and the appropriate reme-dies in detail within Chapter 14 PROBLEM DIAGNOSIS.

I am careful not to spend too much time thinking about all the possible remedies. I choose one and give it a go. I realise I am tinkering and it may not work. If it does not result in an improvement I continue tinkering.

Be sure to think of these things prior to getting near your shot. If you wait until you are standing over the ball, not only will you be playing too slowly but you may be prone to the paralysis through analysis syndrome. Decide what you are going to try before you get to your ball and convince yourself it is the right choice. Then go through your normal pre-shot routine.

An advantage of this tinkering approach is while you have so many positive things to think of and work on, you are focused on remedies and not dwelling on the fact you are having problems. You have then reduced the chance of having the "wheels come off".

If my remedies do not fix my problem I look for another reason such as one of the environmental factors being out of synch (see Section DISCIPLINE later in this chapter), or a playing partner behaving badly, or a very slow round or some factor I have not accounted for.

If I cannot determine the reason, I accept I am having a bad day and this is part of the game of golf. Some days are going to be bad and there is nothing that can be done about it.

If I have too many bad days in a row I go into my correction routine. This involves going back to basics and checking my setup. I accomplish this by performing my bi-weekly drills and spending some time at the practice range if I feel it is necessary.

While performing my correction routine I keep repeating to myself the one point I have learned over the years, that "No matter how much you practice and work there is a delay before the results become apparent." This removes all the pressure from me to get back to form because I know an improvement will come with time. I do not have to push for my game to come back. I also know that pushing and trying too hard will only result in frustration and further poor play.

To keep your confidence up realistic objectives must be set. Unrealistic expectations will destroy your confidence.

If you play infrequently you will be inconsistent. This is a fact of the game of golf. I have heard non-authoritive sources state if you play twice a week you are doing well to get your handicap to 12.

My observations indicate this is generally true. Most people who only play twice a week and have some ability, seem to be in the 12 to 16 handicap range. The exceptions are usually players who once had a much lower handicap and are now playing less frequently.

The most common problem here is the touch and feel with the short game, which is absolutely critical to scoring. This cannot be maintained without frequent playing. Practice just does not seem to be the same.

Do not look at others for your objectives. You may perhaps use their level as an indicator but remember you are a unique individual. If you are not sure what your objectives should be, use the stages within the time frames I experienced as a guideline.

Another pitfall that can adversely affect your confidence is advice. Everyone who plays the game of golf seems eager to offer advice to other players about their faults and how they can improve their game. Be careful as to which advice you accept. Listen to everyone but accept only the comments you believe are valid for you. Most people do not know your game well enough to comment on it and when they do, they may not be correct.

People play the game in many different ways and you need to determine what is best for you with your skills and physical attributes. You may be a Greg Norman type where you hit the ball long and have good touch or you may be the Tom Kite type where you are not overly long but have strengths in all areas or you may be a short hitter who has an excellent short game. Playing with a retired guy who hits the ball only 200 yards (180 metres) off the tee but can get up and down out of a unplayable lie and always shoots between 75 and 78 certainly opened my eyes. Or you may be some combination of these, which most people are. Each player must do what is right for their game.

Also realise that when you are playing well, you may encounter people who are jealous and will attempt to undermine your confidence. They may or may not be intentionally trying to do so, but the result is the same. Most advice though, is usually well meant.

A good measure of your confidence is club selection. If the people you are playing with all hit one or two clubs less than you and you pull out the longer club and do not feel a twinge of wimpiness about it, your confidence is on the proper track.

There are a lot of amateurs out there whose sole purpose seems to be to say they hit a par 5 with a drive and a wedge or used an 8 iron on a long par 3. That is fine for them but do not fall into that trap. The purpose of the game is to score well, no matter which clubs you use. If you have to hit more club than they do to regularly hit your targets, that is the way it is. Accept it.

When playing with the long hitters watch how many more greens they hit than you. Usually these drive and wedge golfers do not hit many greens. If they do and are also getting the ball close, simply accept they are a stronger person than you are and possibly a better golfer. So what? If you are a handicap golfer, there are many people who are physically stronger and better than you are. In fact, no matter who you are there is always someone better than you.

Another test of your confidence is the way you feel when standing on the first tee with a crowd gathered around. All golfers know when they are about to tee off everyone within a radius of twenty miles (kilometres) is watching them, and them only. This is mainly due to etiquette, the crowd is being quiet for your shot. If this does not make you uncomfortable you are on your way. If you do feel uncomfortable just remember every other golfer has been in this position. Most of them understand and sympathise with what you are going through, so just relax and hit away.

If someone hits a bad shot there is usually dead silence from the crowd. This is a form of courtesy to the player who hit the shot and indirectly, an offering of sympathy.

If you do hit a bad shot one reaction is to joke about it and start laughing. Everyone will think you are a nice guy. Possible lines are (with laughter in your voice):

- Good shot Bozo (your name).
- Where did it go? I am long-sighted.
- For a pop up shot, that went further up than forward, I only need to work on the trajectory.
- For a worm burner, won't have trouble finding that one.
- In the bush, I may need to use the foot wedge next, or a machete.
- One putt par coming up.

- While the ball is still moving (if you can react that quickly), talk to the ball with things like go, go, or sit, sit, etc.
- Gee (with surprise in your voice) where did that come from?

Such light-hearted reactions reduce the pressure and help you maintain your confidence by not dwelling on the negative.

Another way to preserve your confidence is to remember you can still recover a par (or a bogey) after just about every bad shot. The exception is when you have hit a ball out of bounds. With the stroke and distance penalty it is very difficult to make par, although not impossible.

On a par 5 where you have hit a short drive it may not cost you anything because you still have four shots to get the ball in the hole for par. Even if you have to take a penalty shot or chip out you still can make par with one or two good shots, or even one good putt.

On the par 4's and 3's you have less room for error on the remaining shots but a par is still possible. Again, maintaining the positive attitude keeps the pressure off and allows you to maintain your confidence.

If you are having a bad day I suggest you play conservatively. Instead of going at tight pin placements aim for the middle of the green, or do not try to cut the corner of a dogleg, etc. Playing conservatively when you are playing poorly will reduce the impact of your poor play on your score.

Confidence is especially important in match play. Never be scared of any opponent, even if you know they are a better player. On any given day you can have a good game and your opponent a bad one. The best golfer does not always win the match. The golfer who played the best during the match usually does.

As I mentioned in Stage 4, the one area where confidence in my whole game is affected is when I am having trouble with short putts. When I am not confident I can make short putts I worry about getting my long putts close, then the pressures expands to my chips, then the wedge shots, then the irons, and eventually I tighten up when I am driving. When I am putting well I know I do not to have to hit every shot perfect and even if I miss a green I can still wedge or chip to within 6 feet (2 metres) most of the time. As long as I am putting well I am confident I can still score well.

Some people let the weather affect their confidence. On a cool and humid day the ball does not fly as far as it would on a warm dry day. Because some do not make the effort to know the weather conditions or they are unaware of the reason for their shots not going as far as usual, they think the problem is with their swing and let it affect their confidence.

A similar thing can happen with course conditions. When the course is in bad shape and a player gets a number of bad lies the results of the shots are not as good as they would be from a good lie. Some question their game because they do not realize the true cause of the problem.

Continually examining my game, finding faults and figuring out solutions to these faults, convinces me I am improving and helps me maintain a positive attitude. Remember improvement in golf involves not only improving the way you hit the ball but also increasing your knowledge of your game.

It is normal to feel doubt, everyone does at one time or another. Believe in yourself. Accept the fact we all hit bad shots and have bad games. Do not let this affect your confidence.

SECTION 11.2 — CONCENTRATION

The second major area of concern when discussing the mental aspects is the ability to concentrate. Concentration is a difficult term to define. One dictionary defines it as "devote all attention". Concentration is more than that to me. It is the ability to block out all distractions and focus total attention on the task of playing the shot.

Good concentration is required for good golf. To play your best you must establish and maintain a high level of concentration.

A common misconception is a player must fully concentrate at all times during the whole round. In other words, be in a "trance" for four hours. Although some people do play like this, not all do. Most players only need to concentrate when deciding how to play the upcoming shot and when playing the shot itself.

When deciding how to play the shot, concentration is required to ensure all the factors that can affect the shot are considered. These include distance, the lie, weather conditions and course management issues. When playing the shot concentration is required to ensure the pre-shot routine is completed, the swing keys are followed and the swing itself is executed properly.

In my case, when I am on the golf course I literally try to enter my own world. I think about the game for the total time. Between shots I may talk to my playing partners, but in the back of my mind I am thinking about the upcoming shot. This is my low level of concentration. As I begin to prepare for my shot I go into a higher level of concentration and maintain this level until I have completed the swing.

When I am concentrating well I feel mentally sharp and keen. My mind is not racing or muddled but calm and clear. I also feel physically relaxed.

When my concentration is good nothing bothers me. I will not hear a jet plane flying over. When my concentration is bad everything bothers me. I will hear my playing partners rattle coins in their pocket from across two fairways.

If I am in a high emotional state or tired I have trouble concentrating. The pace of play can also disrupt my concentration. If the pace is too fast I sometimes end up rushing my routines and my swing. If the pace is too slow I lose the momentum and flow of play.

How I learned to concentrate was I learned not to concentrate on concentrating but to concentrate on my routines. As I played more often, tried hard on every shot and focused on performing my routines, the concentration came naturally. These are described in Chapter 15 ROUTINES AND CHECKLISTS.

What got me started on improving my concentration was a side issue. I realized I was hitting a lot of reasonable shots but these shots were not ending up where I wanted them to. I knew something other than the ability to hit the ball well was involved.

My analysis of each shot indicated I was frequently misaligned, or I would forget to allow for weather conditions, the lie, and other such issues. During the swing I would also forget to think of my swing keys. These errors were caused by simply forgetting to think about them.

My remedy was to enhance my detailed routines and checklists to include all these factors. This gave me a specific sequence of mental tasks to perform for every shot. I would do task A, B, C and so on.

I then exercised the mental discipline to force myself to go through these routines prior to every shot and to think of my swing keys during the execution of the shot.

The repetition of these routines and the mental discipline required to focus on each task within the routines go hand in hand. As I do them more often my concentration improves. Eventually the routines themselves trigger the concentration.

If I am having trouble concentrating due to the pressure of a specific situation I try to concentrate even more. If I succeed great, if I fail I am a choker. Choker may be a bad word, but it communicates the point. For those who do not know, choker is the term given to a person who allows their golf game to deteriorate in pressure situations. I have choked a few times and many times I have performed well under pressure.

While writing this section I have spent many hours thinking about the situations where I played well and the ones where I choked. I do not profess to have the answer to stop myself or anyone else from choking, but my self-analysis did provide me with some insights into my psyche in pressure situations. Perhaps these thoughts will help you figure out how to avoid choking.

I began my analysis of the cause of my choking by reviewing a number of situations. My first thought was I cannot ever remember choking on a 6 foot (2 metre) putt. I have missed a few, but very few. When I HAD to make one of these putts, I made it.

I then thought of a number of shots I made under pressure. I do remember hitting a lot of good shots, but I also remember hitting a few bad shots. I believe I hit more good shots than bad, but this may be due to my tendency to forget the negative and remember the positive.

While thinking through some of my bad shots, the thoughts I remember going through my head at the time were similar to when I feel rushed. My mental thinking sped up and I jumped from one thought to another quickly. I did not finish the previous thought. This caused me to lose concentration and forget steps in my routines.

When I played well my concentration was very good. The times I choked all seemed to be times when my concentration was poor, or it was good and I suddenly lost the good concentration.

I came to the conclusion there were two causes for my loss of concentration. These can occur separately or together. They are:

1. Bad day. Simply one of those days where my concentration was bad.
2. Discomfort. I did not feel comfortable in the situation. After more analysis, I realized that my discomfort came from either of two areas:
   - Confidence. I was not confident I had the skill to execute the shot, or, to complete a round playing at a high level. I did not believe I could achieve the desired result.
   - Insecurity. I did not deserve the result. Beating a good player, shooting a low score or winning a prestigious tournament would take me to a level I felt I did not deserve.

To summarize a complex issue in one sentence: I believe choking is caused by a loss of concentration and that loss of concentration is caused by insecurity or a lack of confidence.

While thinking over the bad shots I had made in past pressure situations I also realised I had made the mistake of assuming some were due to choking and not the real reason, which could be any of the following:

1. Bad shot. Just one of the usual bad shots a player is going to hit. This unfortunately happened to occur in a pressure situation.
2. Wrong shot selection. Trying a shot which was wrong for the situation, such as hitting a long iron out of long grass or off a severe sidehill lie. Today I would not attempt these shots unless they were my only option. Even then if the shot did not come off I would not think I choked, I would just realize they had a low probability of success and the probability came true.

    I did not have the experience and knowledge to choose the correct shot for many situations. It takes time to learn how to play all the predicaments which can arise in this game.
3. Weakness. Trying to hit a shot I do not play well at any time. For example I have trouble hitting my 3 iron and now know this is a weakness of my game. Under pressure I shy away from my 3 iron and usually hit a soft 5 wood instead.

Do not make the mistake of assuming you have choked when the cause of the bad shot is actually one of the reasons above. Incorrectly assuming you have choked can dramatically affect your confidence level, and that can lead to actual choking.

Now to my remedy for choking. To stop the choking I must stop the loss of concentration. Correcting the discomfort is important but in the context of choking, secondary. Discomfort relates to confidence and this has been discussed in the previous section.

I should point out my remedy has worked for me in the past but does not entirely eliminate my choking, it just reduces the number of times I choke. To remedy my loss of concentration requires two steps:

1. Recognition. I must recognize I have lost concentration. This sounds simple but is not always easy to do. Perform some analysis to determine the symptoms you encounter when you have lost concentration. They may or may not be similar to mine. Once you know the symptoms remember to watch for them. When you recognize them, take remedial action. Simple as that. Just being conscious of what to look for will allow you to recognize the condition when it occurs.
2. Mind control. Discipline yourself to get control over your mind and get back into a state of high concentration. To regain control of my

mind I go through the same steps I mentioned earlier. I mentally force myself to think of the appropriate processes at the appropriate time. These are:

- Between shots. Think about the upcoming shot.
- Pre-shot. Mentally focus on my routines and checklists.
- During shot. Mentally focus on my swing keys.

I try not to think about my present score, the score I could shoot, winning the tournament, being considered a good player or the fact I have two putts to win.

The one swing key I follow in pressure situations is hesitate at the top. When I reach the top of the backswing I hold the club there for a second or so and this ensures I do not rush my swing by starting the downswing before I have completed the backswing. Under pressure I sometimes swing too quickly.

Another thing to watch for is the physical aspect. In a pressure situation the adrenalin in your body may increase, causing your body movements to speed up. I can usually solve this by mind control which is discussed earlier in this section and deep breathing exercises. If I breathe deeply a few times and concentrate on my golf game the adrenalin problem goes away.

I also remember times when my hands were shaking and I felt weak all over. I also actually felt fear. I am not sure how I fixed this, I just know it never occurs any more. I suspect it went away when I gained confidence in my ability. I am not afraid of hitting any shot now.

I remember hearing a general comment regarding choking. I believe I heard it in a player interview on television, I am not sure. It is worth repeating. The comment was "You become a regular winner by putting yourself in a position to win. You cannot become a choker unless you have done that. Jack Nicklaus has placed second and third more times than he has won. No one in their right mind would consider him a choker".

There are two messages here. The first is you cannot be in a position to choke unless you have been playing well. If you have choked realize you have reached a new plateau where you need to learn to continue to play well. The second is you cannot win all the time.

These are my comments after my self-analysis on choking. In many cases I was not conscious of the actions I took at the time, but I believe these comments accurately reflect the procedures I have developed over the years. It does not work all the time but it helps. When you lose concentration, or when you are having trouble concentrating, learn to recognize the situation and apply the mental discipline to regain control of your mind. Mentally focus on the appropriate things at the appropriate time.

At my home course I was known as a fierce competitor. The points I have discussed are the major contributing factors.

SECTION 11.3 — DISCIPLINE

By discipline I mean the self-control required to ensure the environmental factors which can affect your game are kept in control. I make a concerted effort to ensure my environmental factors are met as often as possible. They are listed below and will be discussed individually:

1. I must play 18 holes four or more times per week.
2. I must have at least 20 minutes to go through my pre-round routine.
3. The golf course must be in good condition.
4. My mental attitude must be at a positive level — no problems.
5. I must be exercising and watching my diet.
6. I must be doing my bi-weekly drills and practice sessions.
7. My enthusiasm must be high.
8. My golf swing and touch for the short game must be in good but not necessarily great shape.

1. I MUST PLAY 18 HOLES FOUR OR MORE TIMES PER WEEK. I must play frequently to keep my swing and short game tuned. Playing more often would be nice but while holding down a full time job and trying to maintain some semblance of a social calendar, this is all I can generally manage. Discipline applies in ensuring these four or more rounds per week are played.

To accomplish this I set golf at a very high priority when allocating my time. There are a few things I have to sacrifice but if I organise my time correctly I do not lose out on too many. As with scheduling of any resource, it depends on what each individual considers important.

2. I MUST HAVE AT LEAST 20 MINUTES TO GO THROUGH MY PRE-ROUND ROUTINE. I need this time to get into the correct mental frame of mind, loosen my muscles and refamiliarize myself with my swing, putting stroke and chipping touch. The routine I follow is outlined in Chapter 15 ROUTINES AND CHECKLISTS.

Another factor not directly related to my pre-round warmup is the way I schedule my time when I am to play later in the day. If I am at work I try to leave early enough so I do not have to rush to get to the course.

I also prefer not to have any meetings that could drag on at the end of the day, or be at a stage in a work assignment where I am solving a difficult problem. This way I leave work in a positive state of mind and can think about my golf game as I travel to the course.

3. THE GOLF COURSE MUST BE IN GOOD CONDITION. I have heard the touring professionals comment that when the scores are low, the course is in good shape. The way courses are maintained for the average golfer is a pet peeve of mine. I understand it is expensive to keep a course in good condition and the grass cut properly, but I believe these costs should be identified so the dues paying members can choose whether or not to accept the cost. I would be willing to pay far higher fees if I could have a course to play on that was in excellent shape the vast majority of the time.

I firmly believe the overall condition of the course and the regular and proper cutting of the grass affects my scores. I play better in better conditions. Because this makes the game more enjoyable for me, I am willing to spend more money to play.

No matter how much money is spent on a course, the bad areas should be marked as "Ground Under Repair". This is covered in the Rules of Golf and should be adhered to.

I have heard touring professionals say they get five or six bad lies a year on the courses they play on the tour. I have played courses where one third to one half the fairway lies are bad. By bad lies I do not mean the uphill, sidehill lies but how the ball sits on the grass. The best example is where the ball is sitting on bare ground and there is grass behind the ball. These lies make the controlling of the ball impossible even for the very best players.

Another problem is having fairway grass too long. Long fairway grass will cause flyers. Such lies result in lost shots. I have enough trouble with this game without the course itself costing me shots.

It has been argued it is to the better players advantage to have the course in these conditions. I do not accept this argument for the following reasons:

- From a good lie 120 yards (110 metres) from the pin the better player is usually trying to get the ball close to the pin, and will occasionally do so. From a bad lie the better player will probably not get the ball as close, therefore costing a shot every so often. These add up. The poorer player probably would not get the ball close to the pin anyway. The end result is the better player has been penalised and has lost an opportunity to use his skill to get the ball close to the hole. The poorer player has lost nothing.

- A similar, but more self-evident example is where the ball is beside the green, a bunker is between the ball and the pin, and the pin is very close to the edge of the green. Here a delicate touch shot is required to clear the bunker and stop the ball close to the hole.

  This shot is impossible from a bare lie with grass behind the ball, even for the best players. The better player is forced to play a safe shot past the pin, unable to use his superior skill because of the bad lie. The poor player does not have the skill to execute the required shot, so there is no disadvantage to him.

Therefore the only player penalised is the better player. Bad lies take options away from the better players but have a minimal effect on the poorer players. The poorer players do not have the skills to create these options.

A luck element is also introduced because one player may be lucky enough to get a good lie and another a bad lie.

I prefer golf to be a game of skill where a person who has the skills, can use them. I have spent hundreds of hours attaining my skills, and I want the chance to have my score benefit from them.

4.   MY MENTAL ATTITUDE MUST BE AT A POSITIVE LEVEL — NO PROBLEMS. All I'm saying here is I want the world to be a nice place and to have no one hassle me. I understand this is impossible but at least I can reduce hassles.

The most common problem that used to occur was when someone wanted me to do something at a certain time and this conflicted with my golf game. Sometimes I left during a round to meet these commitments. When I chose to finish my round and was late, I got hassled.

I then decided golf was important to me and started telling people I may be late. For some reason quite a few seemed to take this as an insult. They could not accept that playing golf was important to me and I could not adhere to their schedule.

For many, issues like this are not a problem. But if a girlfriend or close friend feels slighted and starts a dispute, something has to be done. The way I learned to handle these nagging problems, is to first explain that golf is my only recreation and it is very important to me.

If that did not satisfy the person I would comment that if I was working instead of playing golf, my priorities would be accepted with no questions asked. It seemed because I was playing golf, many people thought this was a casual thing and my plans could be changed to suit them. Golf was not a casual thing to me.

If I was still being hassled, I would mention they should be happy I was spending my time playing golf and not out drinking and carousing.

Finally, if the dispute continued I would point out that hassling me about how I spend my time shows a lack of consideration for my feelings and wants. Therefore if they are not considerate towards me, I have no obligation to be considerate towards them.

The end result is people accepted my position and began to schedule things around my available time. As it turned out this did not seem to be a major inconvenience. This alleviated any guilt I may have felt when I was out playing and was one less distraction that could disrupt my game.

5. I MUST BE EXERCISING AND WATCHING MY DIET. When I am overweight I feel lethargic and get tired easily.

A side issue here, I am careful about pursuing other hobbies. For example, I will not play tennis frequently because I am worried about overdeveloping my right arm and the muscles on my right side. I am not sure if any overdevelopment would occur but I choose to err on the safe side.

6. I MUST BE DOING MY BI-WEEKLY DRILLS AND PRACTICE SESSIONS. These are discussed in Chapter 15. I perform my drill sequence every second week, sometimes more frequently if I am having problems. The drills take approximately 15 minutes.

At least once every two weeks I have a practice session. What I practice depends on how I am playing at the time. I may decide to go to the driving range and work on full shots or a couple of specific clubs. Or I may decide to go to the practice green and work on my chipping, or putting. Or I may go out on the course when it is not busy and practice sand shots.

If I do not feel any area is particularly weak I practice what I feel like practising. I just make sure I discipline myself to find the time for these sessions every two weeks.

7. MY ENTHUSIASM MUST BE HIGH. Generally enthusiasm is not a problem when I am playing often. I see improvements and this keeps my enthusiasm up. I have gotten stale with golf but only after playing ten days in a row, and 36 holes on some of these days.

To rekindle my enthusiasm all I have to do is take two or three days off. This is the only cure I know, get away from the game for awhile.

Related to enthusiasm is the people I am to play the round with. There are very few people I do not like to play golf with. It comes down to the way they handle themselves on the course. I admit a preference for playing with better players but a high handicapper who does the correct things is quite acceptable. Things that playing partners can do that annoy me are:

7.1. IGNORE ETIQUETTE. Walk on my putting line, do not rake bunkers or replace divots, etc.

7.2. TALK TOO MUCH. In the four hours it takes to play a round of golf there is a lot of time to chat. This is okay, but there is a line here that is hard to define. I am on the course to play golf, not socialise. Some talking is good, but too much can get on my nerves.

Part of this is the time the people talk. Between shots is all right but when I get near my ball I want to be able to prepare for my shot in peace.

7.3. NEGATIVE VIBES. Some people totally change character when they play golf. They become abusive, use foul language (excessive) and In effect bother the other players. I understand someone getting angry occasionally and blowing off steam, I have been there many times myself, but constant and extreme bad behaviour bothers me.

Another form of negative vibes is the person who runs down everybody else's golf game. They never say "good shot" and always point out any lucky breaks you get. They also openly criticize aspects of other players games. I prefer to play with people who are positive and cheer each other on.

I also do not like to play with teammates who make comments about your playing badly. When I am playing badly I know it and am probably a little angry about it myself. I do not need to be hassled about it.

Many years ago, when my handicap was 19 I played in a two day tournament. My confidence in my golf game was not high and I was unsure of how to conduct myself in these tournaments. As will happen, I did not play well in the first round.

After the round, two of my team members took great pains to point out how bad a golfer I was. I was quite embarrassed. I just sat in the clubhouse and took it. My reaction would be entirely different now, but back then I left determined to play better the next day. I figured I would show those jerks.

The next morning I came out keen and determined. I hardly talked to my teammates, I just concentrated on playing golf. I managed to make a few putts and shoot a good score. I was happy, especially since both the other guys did not play well.

When I got to the clubhouse I sat with some other people and ignored my teammates. For years I made an effort to avoid these guys. Petty? maybe, but they should have known better.

Many high handicappers are uncomfortable with their golf games and can get upset easier than people who have a lower handicap and have been playing the game for years. Most try very hard to play their best in tournaments and it is up to the lower handicappers to take care of them. All that is required here is being cheerful and offering encouragement.

Today if I was in a tournament and playing badly with my team members hassling me, I would either walk off the course (a real insult) or purposely begin to play as bad as I could. If I continued to play I would also be sure to laugh at my bad shots. I am sure this would aggravate the jerks.

7.4. HIGH STAKES. I believe playing golf for a small amount of money can add an incentive to do well and increase the enjoyment of the game. The problem is people who are betting more than they are comfortable with. The amount varies with each individual, but if they become too serious and uptight the stakes are too high.

The largest bet I have ever made was $100 for low medal score over 18 holes. Both my opponent and myself could afford this and were comfortable with it. We had a very good game. It came down to the 18th green where my opponent had to make a tricky sidehill 4 foot (1.2 metre) putt to tie. I had just made a straight uphill 5 foot (1.8 metre) putt. I will not tell you whether he made it or not, but I will say he hit a very good putt.

Generally I like to only play for a few dollars. Anything more than that and I get annoyed if I lose.

8. MY GOLF SWING AND TOUCH FOR THE SHORT GAME MUST BE IN GOOD BUT NOT NECESSARILY GREAT SHAPE. This is the last of my critical environment factors. One may think it is the most important factor but I do not think so. I have come to the conclusion I do not need to be hitting the ball very well to score well. This is why I chose the words "good but not necessarily great". To score well I must be able to get the ball in the hole. A one putt par is still a par.

For me, just playing four times a week and going through my drills and routines is usually enough to keep my game at a reasonable level. I suspect this is due to the lengthy learning process I have gone through.

It is important I discipline myself to ensure these environmental factors are in place. This may not always be possible but I make a major effort to keep them in the proper state. In some ways this requires being a little selfish.

I suggest you determine the environmental factors that affect you and do all you can to ensure they are met. Being aware of, and eliminating or reducing any problems, will help improve your on course performance.

SECTION 11.4 — TEMPERAMENT

Golf is a game of self-control, discipline and above all a mastering of the emotions. I cannot remember where I heard this, but it certainly is true.

Emotion, be it positive (elation) or negative (anger) is a part of the game. Even the touring professionals admit to experiencing emotions while playing. I have heard a number of them talk about their need to flatten out the emotional roller coaster they experience during some rounds.

For me, it is beyond my ability to eliminate reacting to emotion. I simply am not objective about my playing of the game. I care. Examples of emotion on the course are:

- I swing hard at my tee shot because I bogeyed the last hole.
- I speed up my routine because I am angry.
- I get sloppy with a shot from the fairway because I hit a drive further than I ever hit a drive before.

The key to handling emotions is the diffusing of the emotion before I hit my next shot. From the time I have hit the good or the bad shot I allow myself to experience the emotion. By the time I begin to prepare for my next shot, hopefully I have diffused this emotion, or at least have it under a level of control.

How I adjust to my emotions depends on the emotion I am experiencing. I must also point out that what I am about to say does not always work. There are times my emotions get the better of me.

If I am elated or excited because I am playing well, I try to mentally slow myself down and relax. While I am walking to my ball I take deep breaths, do some stretching exercises and may even jog down the fairway. The physical exertion helps me relax.

When excited I like to talk a lot. If I am playing with people I do not know well I walk down the side of the fairway away from them and talk to myself. Nobody listens, or cares anyways so why not. This is a way of helping me calm down.

When in this state I also slow down my pre-shot routine in order to focus my concentration. I do not slow it down much, just enough to ensure I am not quick with the routine. As in pressure situations, I set myself a swing key of hesitating at the top of my backswing so I do not get too fast with the swing. I have a tendency to swing too fast when excited.

Above all when I am playing well and excited I allow myself to enjoy the feeling. This is what I am out there for.

Anger is another emotion which has a potentially damaging impact on my game. I accept I am going to hit a number of bad shots and that is not usually what makes me angry. I get angry when I hit stupid shots or do stupid things. Examples of situations where I am likely to get angry are:

- I take the wrong club out of my bag by mistake, and do not notice it before I hit the shot.
- I leave a putt 4 feet (1.1 metres) short and decide to putt out without properly lining up. If I miss the next putt I am not happy.
- I double bogey a hole.
- I dump a short wedge shot into a bunker.
- I know I am not aligned properly when I am over a shot and do not stop to correct it.
- I know I have the ball teed too high and still hit the shot. If I tee the ball too high I will probably hit a snap hook.
- I simply forget to adjust for some factor I know exists. An example is not allowing enough for a strong wind when I am in the middle of the round.
- Trying a foolish recovery shot which I should know better than to try, but was just hoping it would come off. There is a line here. Usually I analyse the risks of the shot and decide to accept them or not. If it turns out bad I accept it. It is when I convince myself to hit a no-hoper and it inevitably has a bad result, it bothers me.
- I have just hit my limit of bad shots for the day. This limit varies, but generally I am playing poorly and my diagnostic routines are not solving my problem. A better word is frustration not anger.
- I hit my second shot on a par 5 into trouble, especially if I am laying up.
- Having a shot catch a tree which I should have allowed for and played around. I do not mean as the result of an errant shot but one within reasonable expectations.
- Uncut grass on the course and poor conditions.
- The person keeping score asks me three times what my score was on the last hole, when I made double bogey.

When I get angry I may scowl, and even cuss (quietly most of the time). After a shot there is always a slight delay until the next player is ready to hit and this gives me time to react without bothering anyone else.

I may even throw a club. I do not mind playing with people who throw clubs as long as it is thrown in the correct manner. Be aware though, some people feel uncomfortable being around players who throw clubs, no matter how they do it. To throw a club properly requires the following sequence:

1. Ready. Look around to ensure no one is preparing to hit or in your vicinity. This action in itself is usually enough to diffuse my initial burst of anger. If anyone is preparing for a shot or anywhere near you, abort the throw, repeat abort the throw.

2. Aim. Choose a direction to throw the club. Allow a large margin for error here as the club may slip out of your hand or you may hang onto it longer than you want. BE SURE NO ONE IS ANYWHERE NEAR THE TARGET AREA. Also watch for golf bags, power carts, etc. You may end up having to pay for a new paint job on a power cart — serves you right! Also watch for trees and bushes where the club could get hung up.

   It is recommended you throw the club in the direction you are planning to go. This saves the time it takes to walk back and pick it up.

3. Fire. Gently toss the club in your chosen direction. Tossing the club gently will eliminate the chance of the club being thrown off target. I usually drop the club on the ground or toss it a few feet (metres) to my bag. This is usually enough to diffuse the highest level of my anger.

4. Retrieve. Proceed to pick up the club, clean it and put it in your bag. I repeat, I do not condone wild club throwing. I have actually had a club spin around me, thrown by a guy who just missed a short putt. I told him if he ever did that again I would refuse to play with him.

Perhaps the best policy is to not throw clubs. It is not worth the possible consequences. Clubs can bounce in an erratic manner when they land, or they can ricochet off bags, trees, etc. You do not want to injure anyone, including yourself. You could also be eligible for a law suit if you hit someone.

The best way I have found to diffuse my anger after a bad hole, is to toss the ball away as I walk to the next tee. I ensure I toss the ball to an area where no one is near. Water hazards or bushes are a good place. If this is done in a proper manner, after all players have finished the hole, it can be humorous.

When playing with someone I do not know, I usually get a funny look when they see me do this. I smile, shrug, and say "That ball is no good, too many double bogeys in it." This can be very non-threatening even to a very sensitive person if handled properly. It is all in the smile and the shrug.

This method also has a financial incentive for me to play better. Golf balls are not cheap and if I keep throwing them away my expenses go up. I justify this by reminding myself I did not play well with the ball, so I may as well get rid of it. I could save these balls and put them in my practice bag, but I do not. I enjoy the feeling of throwing the ball away. These actions help me diffuse the emotions I am feeling at the time. Many times just walking to my next shot is enough. While approaching the ball I begin my routine and this helps me focus on the next shot and forget about the last. If I am really angry I remind myself that a shot hit in anger is probably a shot (or more) lost.

The calmer and cooler you are the higher the probability you can concentrate on your next shot and the higher the probability of your hitting a good shot. A shot hit is history. No matter what you say, do or think, the shot has been hit and the result will not change. Accept it as part of the game and work on your next shot. Be positive, you may be able to recover and still save par, or bogey.

If I am in a blind rage the above actions will not work. But I can honestly say I do not ever remember being so angry I could not think through my actions. If I ever reached a point on the golf course where I lost total control I believe it would be time to give up the game. Minor expressions of frustration and anger are okay, blind rage no.

Another point here regarding temperament, is the general vibes you give off to the others in your group. If you are pleasant, easy going and positive they are more likely to be the same. This makes for pleasant golf and an enjoyable time.

Always make an effort to encourage your playing partners. If they hit a good shot, compliment them. Even if you are four down with four holes left be pleasant. You are out here for a hobby, it is not life or death.

You should never give up on a round. Although I have done so at times, I believe if you keep trying you will learn something every round. I know this is hard when you are ten over par after a few holes, but keep going.

If the score is totally gone, turn the round into a practice round. Change your target areas to give yourself shots you do not normally have. For example, aim at bunkers or use a different club off the tee. Be innovative to keep your interest up. These things pay off in the long run.

I am a competitive person. When I get upset with my game I am driven to improve. I care how I perform. Without this caring, or passion, I would not make the effort to improve. I see this passion in many of the touring professionals, although theirs is at a higher level than mine (maybe).

This passion, harnessed into determination and concentration can be very positive and productive. It is when this passion is destructive and ruins the concentration, that problems occur. Unfortunately most of us have to experience the destructive side before we learn the productive side. Some never do and never will.

Do not feel too bad if you are at the destructive stage. Accept this as a natural evolution and work on turning it into a productive force.

In summary try to be pleasant, positive and easy going. Above all be considerate of your playing partners. If things are going very well and you get excited, calm yourself down. If you are angry and frustrated find a quiet non-threatening, non-obtrusive way to diffuse these emotions before you hit your next shot.

SECTION 11.5 — GAMESMANSHIP

Gamesmanship is the use of comments and intimidation with the purpose of adversely affecting an opponent's performance. It is also known as playing mind games.

I believe using gamesmanship is an admission of inferior ability. People who use it regularly do not believe they can beat you with their golf game by itself, so they think they must use mind games. When faced with gamesmanship try to recognize it for what it is and not let it affect your game.

I have used gamesmanship in the past but now prefer not to. Golf is enough of a mental game and after awhile I find the mind games tiring.

The only time I will use gamesmanship, is when I am absolutely sure someone is trying to use it on me. I give the person every benefit of the doubt because I understand golf is an emotional game and people may say things in the heat of the competition which they do not mean to be gamesmanship.

If I am totally convinced after a number of incidents that someone is trying to play mind games, I will give it back. I have a number of tactics I use which are subtle and also subject to multiple interpretations so that no one can accuse me of playing the games.

I will not discuss my tactics here because I do not condone the use of them. Nevertheless, it is important that you be able to recognize gamesmanship when it is being used. This way you can understand what is going on and ignore it. Or if you choose, respond to it.

The best source I have seen for the possible games is the book "THE CHEAT'S GUIDE TO GOLF" by Colin Bowles, published by Angus and Robertson. I recommend this book. It is not only informative, it is interesting and very funny.

CHAPTER 12
WEATHER FACTORS

This chapter describes the adjustments required based on specific weather conditions. Every round of golf is played in some type of weather. You need to know how to adapt your game to the conditions.

The weather factors that can affect your score include temperature, wind, relative humidity, rain, and light.

To show how serious an issue I feel weather factors are, I am the only person I know who took the time to call the local weather office prior to a round. They provide a recorded message giving the temperature, wind direction and velocity, relative humidity and the amount of rainfall.

I got the idea from a pilot who joined our group one day. He mentioned the weather office provided this service and gave me the number to call. I did not tell anyone at first because I was worried if too many people knew the number they would tie up the line and I couldn't get through. I soon learned that few people are interested enough to make the call. Too bad for them. I now check the weather channel on cable for the information.

Knowing the exact weather conditions is important and can save shots. Weather can dramatically affect the flight of the ball, both in the distance it will travel and the amount it may be moved offline. Being aware of the exact conditions allows the effect to be predicted at the beginning of the round rather than later after a number of shots have been played and the effects have become apparent.

For example, knowing the exact wind velocity, direction and relative humidity allows me to predict the effect the wind will have on a shot on the first hole. Adjusting correctly can make the difference between being on the green or in a bunker. In the long run, such knowledge and the ability to make the proper adjustments will reduce your score.

SECTION 12.1 — TEMPERATURE
The two main issues to consider with temperature are the effect on the distance the ball will travel and the impact on your swing of your clothing and muscles.

SUBSECTION 12.1.1 — PERFECT WEATHER
For me, perfect golf weather is a temperature of 73 to 76 degrees Fahrenheit (22 to 25 degrees Celsius), little or no wind and low relative humidity (30 to 50%). This is comfortable shirt sleeve weather.

I use the distance I hit the ball in perfect weather as my foundation for club selection. The distances I hit my clubs are listed below. These are for carry only (distance in the air), as the amount the ball rolls depends on how wet the ground is, the terrain, whether it hits a tree or not, and other non-climatic circumstances. These are also based on the flight of the ball at an elevation of 2100 feet (670 metres) above sea level.

Sand Wedge	Up to 100 yards (90 meters).
Pitching Wedge	Up to 115 yards (105 meters).
9 Iron	120 to 125 yards (109 to 114 meters).
8 Iron	130 to 135 yards (119 to 123 meters).
7 Iron	140 to 145 yards (128 to 133 meters).
6 Iron	150 to 155 yards (137 to 142 meters).
5 iron	160 to 165 yards (146 to 151 meters).
4 Iron	170 to 175 yards (155 to 160 meters).
3 Iron	180 to 185 yards (165 to 169 meters).
5 Wood	200 to 210 yards (183 to 192 meters).
4 Wood	210 to 220 yards (192 to 201 meters).
3 Wood	205 to 220 yards (187 to 201 meters).
Driver	200 to 220 yards (183 to 201 meters).

These distances assume I am playing well, in mid-season form and are for a shot hit with my normal full swing. They are not the distances when I hit the ball hard or soft.

The terms hard and soft are hard to define. Normally I hit a shot at about 70 percent of full power. By full power I mean swinging as hard as I can. I can swing at about 85 percent of full power and be comfortable I will maintain my balance. So 70 percent of full power is about 80 percent of full power with balance. A hard swing is about 15 percent harder than a normal swing but not hard enough to threaten a loss of balance. A soft swing is about 15 percent easier than a normal swing.

I do not have any scientific measurement of the difference. The variance in the force of the swing feels to be about 15 percent to me. The hard or soft swing changes the range of the shot by approximately 5 yards (4 metres) each way, assuming constant weather conditions.

When professional golfers quote their ranges, the distances are usually between 10 and 15 yards (9 and 13 metres). I suspect they are including soft and hard shots, I have just broken it down into more categories.

You need to know how far you hit your clubs in all temperatures. Pick a temperature and determine the foundation distances you hit each club at that temperature. Use these numbers as a base to adjust to the varying conditions.

SUBSECTION 12.1.2 — COOL AND COLD WEATHER

Cool weather is 50 to 72 degrees Fahrenheit (10 to 21 degrees Celsius) and cold weather is from 35 to 49 degrees Fahrenheit (2 to 9 degrees Celsius). Very cold weather is below these temperatures.

I have played in the very low 30's Fahrenheit (minus 1 Celsius). This is no fun. Call it dedication or stupidity, your choice. However anyone who wishes to play golf seriously in Edmonton, Canada must be prepared to play in cold weather.

The effects of the cold on one's golf game are many. The colder the weather the more apparent these effects become.

The first adjustment is to allow for the ball not to fly as far. Cold air is denser than warm air so there is more resistance while the ball is in flight.

The second adjustment is with the swing. Depending on your individual body and the way you are dressed, your swing will be somewhat restricted. At cold temperatures the muscles are stiffer than they would be at a warmer temperature. My back and shoulder muscles tighten up, resulting in a less than normal shoulder turn.

In cold weather I wear multiple layers of clothing. On a very cold day I wear wool underwear (long johns), a wool t-shirt, a cotton turtleneck with long sleeves, a golf shirt and a sweater. For the sweater I prefer a velour material with a zipper in front so I can quickly unzip it before a shot and reduce some of the binding from the clothes.

I may wear a wool hat and mittens to keep my hands warm between shots. Mittens are warmer than gloves because the fingers are together.

I also keep DEEP HEAT ™ liniment in my locker and prior to a round on very cold days I put some on my lower back. This helps the back and shoulders loosen up quicker and stay loosened up. By the time it wears off I have been walking for a few holes and my back and shoulders are as loose as they are going to get.

The end result of tighter muscles and cumbersome clothing is a loss of distance and a different swing than my normal swing. I change my tempo by slowing it down.

When it is cold I reduce my pre-round warmup session by hitting fewer putts and chips. I still do my stretching exercises and in fact may do a few extra just before starting my round. If there is time to wait before the tee time I spend it in the pro shop getting warm.

The performance characteristics of golf balls change in very cold weather. Certain brands feel hard when hit, do not pick up the normal amount of spin and are very hard to control with chipping. A professional once suggested I use two balls during the round exchanging them on every other hole. The ball not in use was to be kept in my pocket to warm it up. The result was to be more distance and control with the ball. Sometimes I do this, sometimes not.

In cool weather I try not to bundle up too much. I wear a t-shirt, a golf shirt and my zippered sweater. The sweater can be unzipped or taken off quickly for a shot. I also like a sweater to have loose sleeves so I can pull them up to my elbows if I am too warm.

When I start a round in cool weather I use one club more on each shot. In cold weather two clubs more. I then watch the results of my shots and continue to adjust during the round.

Cool weather has the same effect as cold weather but not to the same extent. Each person must play in the varying weather conditions and learn the adjustments required based on their specific game.

SUBSECTION 12.1.3 — HOT AND VERY HOT WEATHER

Hot weather is 77 to 90 degrees Fahrenheit (25 to 32 degrees Celsius), with very hot being above these temperatures. In hot temperatures the ball will travel farther, your muscles will be looser and the ball may change its playing characteristics.

The main adjustment in hot weather is allowing for the ball to fly further. This is due to two reasons. Hot air is not as dense as cold air with the effect being less resistance, and a warm ball will travel farther.

I require a different swing for hot weather than for cold. In hot temperatures my shoulders, back and leg muscles loosen up so much that unless I make a conscious effort to hold my swing together I feel my swing is out of control.

I accomplish this by tensing the muscles, which is not easy to describe. I start by turning my arm muscles a bit but not so much as to restrict my swing. I then shift my upper and lower body around by twisting slightly until the appropriate muscles feel right. To determine the correct amount of tension you have to try it.

The differences in the required swings became apparent one autumn when I travelled to Las Vegas. In Edmonton the weather was cool to cold and my swing was a cool weather one. The weather in Vegas was hot and I noticed the difference in my swing. I had to make the above adjustments.

I also tend to bend over the ball a little more in hot weather and stand a little more upright in cold weather.

In hot weather I wear a loose golf shirt, light colored trousers (or better yet, shorts) and always a hat. A large hat with a brim to provide as much shade as possible.

When starting a round in hot weather I use my normal club distances and swing easy. In very hot weather I take one club less and swing easy. I then watch the results and adjust accordingly.

SECTION 12.2 — RELATIVE HUMIDITY

Relative humidity is the percentage of water vapour in the air relative to the amount of water vapour the air can hold. The vapour holding capacity of the air varies at different temperatures.

Relative humidity is important in relation to the temperature and the wind. With temperature, I ignore the humidity if it is less than 80 percent. If the humidity is 80 percent or greater I move the temperature category down one, for example from very hot to hot when deciding on the adjustment for club selection.

With the wind, I consider the relative humidity only if it is 50 percent or higher. When the humidity is under 50 percent the wind does not affect the ball as significantly. The adjustments to the wind strength based on the relative humidity are discussed in the WIND Section later in this chapter.

I have heard it said by some that when the humidity is high the ball flies further. That may be true for them. For me, when the humidity is high the ball does not fly as far. Of this, I am sure. The reason for the difference may be the normal idiosyncrasies between golfers. They may hit the ball harder and higher than me or the type of ball they use may cause the difference. What is important is that you are aware of the humidity and determine how it affects your shots.

The humidity in the air can also affect your ability to judge distances. If you make distance judgements by sight you should be aware when the humidity is high, dust and other particles in the air are reduced. This has the result of making objects, like the pin, appear closer. When the humidity is low there are more particles in the air which obscure your vision and make objects appear further away.

Knowing the relative humidity allows me to properly gauge the effect of the temperature and the wind on the flight of the ball. A correct adjustment can make the difference between a shot ending up on the green or stymied behind trees. A round of 75 turned into a 77 simply because I did not allow for the relative humidity.

SECTION 12.3 — RAIN
By rain I mean a steady flow, not a light mist.

Many people say they play their best in the rain. There are a number of possible reasons with two main ones. The first is water between the ball and the clubface reduces the amount of spin imparted to the ball, both backspin and sidespin. Therefore the ball will fly straighter.

The second main reason is psychological. Because the weather is bad players accept that they are going to score higher. They ease up, reducing the pressure on themselves and concentrate on just trying to hit the ball. This relaxation allows them to play better.

Another reason is there is less roll on the course, both on the fairway and on the greens. A tee shot that would run into trouble in dry conditions may stop short in wet conditions. A wet green may hold shots that would have rolled over the back on a dry green. These can all result in a better score.

When playing in the rain I generally use one more club and swing easy. I do so for three reasons; the loss of distance due to the resistance of the moisture in the air, water getting between the clubface and the ball and the reduced roll on the course, as mentioned earlier.

I also reduce the times I intentionally try to curve the ball because it is more difficult to do so and I may change my target areas, again due to the reduced roll on the course. If I have taken a practice swing and the clubface is wet, I wipe it before hitting the shot.

When the greens are wet I can fly my shots near the pin and the ball will stop quicker and more consistently. With chip shots I like wet greens because I am very accurate where I can land the ball and I seem to get a more predictable result.

Wet greens are slower and have less break which can make them easier to putt. The effect on the break depends on how wet the green is. A light rain will not make a big difference but if the green is soaked there will be a noticeable reduction in the break. On very wet greens long putts may aquaplane for some distance.

The disadvantage of wet greens is footprints do not recover as quickly and if there has been a lot of traffic they can get quite bumpy.

On a rainy day I usually wear my rainsuit which includes a jacket and pants. If you play a lot in the rain and do not own one I suggest you buy one. A good rain suit will keep you dry and comfortable.

I usually carry an umbrella and keep a towel on the spokes because I have seen a number of touring professionals carry their towel in this manner.

I also cover the top of the golf bag to stop the water from running down inside the bag and getting the grips wet. If the cover that came with your golf bag is not large enough, buy a cover. Either one for just the top of the bag or one for the whole bag, your choice.

Earlier I mentioned I would dry the clubface before I made a shot. This is not always true. In the case of an iron shot I would. However on the tee I usually do not wipe the clubface because the moisture will reduce the sidespin, causing the ball to fly straighter. I will not deliberately wet the clubface, for example by taking practice swings in wet grass or hold the club out with the clubface upward so the rain will land on it, but I will not walk to my bag and wipe it. I have seen many other players doing this.

The problem is the Rules of Golf specifically prohibit the applying of foreign material to the clubface in order to influence the movement of the ball. My interpretation is if a player deliberately wets the clubface he is guilty of a breach of the rule. If the player goes through his normal routine he is not guilty. There is no rule requiring a player to clean the clubface.

A reminder here. Where there is rain there may be lightning. Watch for it and get off the course if there is danger. Lightning kills, do not make this your last round of golf.

As with the other weather factors mentioned in this chapter, knowing the effect rain will have on your game and making the proper adjustments will improve your scoring. In summary, when it is wet take one more club, swing easy and do not try to hit fancy (curving) shots.

SECTION 12.4 — WIND

Playing golf in a strong wind is difficult. When the wind blows the scores go up, even for the professionals.

I find playing in the wind very interesting. I treat every full shot in the wind as a trouble shot. By this I mean I carefully plan the shot before I execute it.

I have had some of my best games in the wind. I once shot 75 at my home course in a 50 mile (80 kilometre) per hour wind. This was a very good score in difficult conditions. I was upset after the round because I hit a bad chip on the 18th green which caused me to take three shots to get down from 20 feet (6 metres). I felt I deserved a 74 and only missed it because I was careless with a chip shot. Still, I remember this round as one of my best.

How the ball is affected by the wind depends on the following factors:
1. SPEED, RELATIVE HUMIDITY AND TEMPERATURE OF THE WIND. A strong, wet, cold wind will affect the ball more than a weak, dry, hot wind.

A weak wind is less than 10 miles (16 kilometres) per hour. A moderate wind is 10 to 20 miles (17 to 32 kilometres) per hour and a strong wind more than 20 miles (32 kilometres) per hour. These definitions assume the temperature is warm (72 degrees Fahrenheit (22 degrees Celsius)) and the relative humidity is 50 percent or less.

If the temperature is higher than 72 degrees Fahrenheit (22 degrees Celsius) drop the category of the wind down one, for example from moderate to weak. If the temperature is lower than 72 degrees OR the relative humidity is higher than 50 percent, move the wind category up one, for example weak to moderate. If the temperature is below 50 degrees Fahrenheit (10 degrees Celsius) AND the relative humidity is over 50 percent, move the category up one more.
2. DIRECTION. Is the wind into, behind, across or at an angle to your line of play. On the course this can be difficult to determine. You may be surrounded by trees and therefore sheltered from the wind. Or you may be playing in an area where the wind is swirling due to the funnelling and shielding effects (see point 6 below). To determine the direction of the wind I look at the following:

- The direction the flag on the pin is pointing. This will tell me the direction of the wind at the green.
- The direction the tops of nearby trees are moving.
- Grass clippings tossed in the air. This will tell me the direction of the wind where I am standing. If I am in the middle of the fairway and there are no trees or other shields from the wind, the direction indicated will probably hold for the length of the hole.
- I mentioned earlier I always called the weather office prior to a round. One of the pieces of information gained from this call was the wind direction. I assume the direction received from the weather office is still correct if I do not have strong evidence from the points mentioned here to convince me otherwise. During the

course of a round it is unusual for the wind to change direction more than a little. But it can happen.

- The flag on top of my home course clubhouse. This flag is at a high point and whenever I am in a position to see the flag I check the direction it is pointing.
- If I am not the first person to hit I watch the flight patterns of other shots. To make an accurate assessment of the wind based on someone else's shot requires me to know their normal flight patterns. If someone normally hits a draw and their shot draws this is not necessarily due to the wind. Only watch those shots that are hit well. A poor weak shot will be affected more by the wind. Here is an advantage of playing with consistent players, you can gain information from their shots which help to determine the adjustments you must make.

Different wind directions can dramatically change the difficulty of a course and the manner in which it should be played. A hole may be difficult with the wind from one direction and easy when the wind comes from another direction. The direction of the wind can also change your target areas for the hole. Some examples are:

- Into the wind you may not be able to reach a group of trees, but with the wind they are in range.
- Into the wind you may be able to fly a long iron into a green and stop the ball quickly. With the wind you may not be able to stop the ball at all on the green. This may force you to place your drive in a position which lets you run the ball onto the green.
- With the wind you land the ball past fairway bunkers. Against the wind you may land in an area which kicks the ball into a bunker.

My rule of thumb for a moderate headwind (directly into my face) is add one club for an approach shot to the green (take a 6 instead of a 7 iron). For a strong headwind take two clubs more. I will usually ignore a weak wind, or at the most make a small adjustment, perhaps hitting a shot normal rather than soft.

My rule of thumb for a weak assisting tailwind is to ignore it. For a moderate or strong tailwind I take one club less and allow for a little more roll. With an assisting wind I may hit a 3 wood off the tee for extra height to increase the distance of the shot.

A strong crosswind can move the ball a long way off the initial flight path. The distance the ball is moved depends on a multitude of factors. These include the time the ball is in the air, how well the ball is hit, the dimple pattern of the ball, the velocity, temperature and humidity of the wind and any swirling conditions.

For a crosswind I adjust my target area by the amount I think the ball will be moved and hit the usual club. The exception is if I am going to fade or draw the ball into or against the wind. If the ball is going to fly with the direction of the wind, for example fade a shot with a left to right crosswind, I hit the same club but hit it soft. If I am going to curve the shot against the wind I go down a club and hit the shot soft.

If the wind is angled I make an adjustment based on what I feel is proper. I do not have a formula here, I just do what I think is right. If the wind is more of a headwind than a crosswind I allow for a higher percentage effect from the headwind portion and a lower percentage for the crosswind. If the wind is more of a crosswind I allow more for the ball to be moved sideways, but still allow some for the headwind.

In other words, a wind coming from one o'clock will hold the ball up somewhat but not as much as a direct headwind coming from 12 o'clock. A wind coming from two o'clock will move the ball sideways but not as much as if the wind was from three o'clock. On both these shots the ball will also be affected by the secondary factor but to a lesser extent than the primary factor. Things like this make the game fun. Or at least interesting.

It takes experience to learn to judge the effects of the wind. On the course watch your shots and the shots of your playing partners to make your adjustments. Early in the round make your best guess based on the exact conditions you have obtained from the weather office and your past experience.

3.   THE HEIGHT OF THE SHOT AND THE SPEED THE BALL IS MOVING. Most of the effect of the wind occurs at the end of the flight of the ball. To illustrate, watch a shot hit with the driver. As the ball comes off the clubface at a reasonably fast speed there is no effect from the wind. The real effect becomes noticeable after the shot has reached its pinnacle and begins to drop to the ground.

A 9 iron shot is more susceptible to the wind than a 3 iron shot because the trajectory of the 3 iron shot is lower. The higher the shot the longer it takes to come down, therefore the higher shot is exposed to the wind longer while it is travelling at a slower speed.

When faced with a short iron shot with a strong headwind, crosswind or angled wind I usually hit a boring punch shot. This shot is far less affected by the wind than a high short iron shot.

The punch shot is a low flying shot which requires a special technique. To hit a punch play the ball back 1 or 2 inches (2 to 5 centimetres) in your stance and do not release your wrists as your bring the club through the hitting area. Once mastered, this shot is a great tool.

When hitting a punch shot I take one more club and swing softly. In other words, if I am at a distance which is a normal 8 iron from the target and there is a moderate headwind (add one club because of moderate headwind, now at 7 iron) and decide to play a punch shot, I will hit a soft 6 iron punch (add one more club again because of a punch shot).

With these adjustments in club selection there is some overlap. For example in cold weather (add 2 clubs), into a strong wind (add 2 more) when hitting a punch shot (add 1 more) the actual result is not to add 5 clubs, but I add at least 2 and possibly 3 clubs depending on the situation.

The key being the number of adjustments required. If just one adjustment is required I make the full adjustment. If multiple factors are involved I decide based on past experience and what I think is right. Experiment and you will learn the correct adjustments for your game.

I once happened to see Jack Nicklaus on the practice tee before a round on a windy day. The wind was blowing directly across (90 degrees from right to left). I noticed he watched the flight of his shots very carefully to see the amount the wind was moving them. You should watch the effect of the wind on all your shots during the round and continue to adjust accordingly.

4.   THE AMOUNT OF BACKSPIN AND SIDESPIN ON THE BALL. The more backspin the higher the ball will fly, unless you are using a ball with a low trajectory dimple pattern. You may even get the balloon effect where the ball reaches a point in its trajectory where it climbs almost straight up and drops straight down with the result of a significant loss of distance.

Hitting a shot hard imparts extra backspin increasing the risk of the balloon effect. The balloon effect can also occur when the ball is curved into a crosswind.

Downwind and off the tee, more backspin may be desirable because the higher the ball flies the more the wind will carry it and the further the shot will go. Into the green, an assisting wind will reduce the backspin so allow for extra roll.

Sidespin is a disaster in a strong headwind. The headwind will exaggerate the amount of curve the ball will take. Downwind the amount of curve will be reduced.

With a crosswind the effect depends on the direction of the curve of the ball. If the ball curves into the crosswind the amount of curve will be less and the distance the ball travels is reduced. When hitting a shot into a green this type of shot can be used to stop the ball quickly.

Curving the ball in the same direction as the crosswind will exaggerate the amount the ball will curve. Into a green, the ball will roll more. If you need to move the ball around an object, a crosswind can be used to increase the curving of the shot.

5.   THE TYPE OF BALL. Certain brands definitely hold the line better in the wind. There are also balls on the market designed to produce a low trajectory which is a plus in the wind.

Reports in golf magazines state surlyn-covered balls spin less than balata-covered balls when hit with the same club and force. Less backspin and sidespin is an advantage when playing in the wind.

6.   THE WIND PATTERNS ON THE COURSE. This is the funnelling, shielding and wind-shear effects of hills, trees and buildings.

The funnelling effect is the result of wind being compacted into a smaller area, creating a stronger wind. The shielding effect is the blocking of the wind resulting in a weaker or totally non-existent wind. The wind-shear (or turbulence) effect is caused by air passing over hills and valleys resulting in a wind that is bouncing vertically up and down. In some areas this wind-shear is strong enough to affect airplanes.

To play in the wind effectively you must analyse the surrounding terrain and buildings to determine where these conditions will occur. You must also consider the different directions of the wind.

It may be too difficult to figure out all the possible effects when the wind blows from all possible directions, but you should at least look at the possibilities based on the prevailing winds in your area.

Things to look for here are:

- Gaps in tree lines. Trees, depending on the type, are usually a good shield. Where a gap exists watch for the funnel effect.
- Above trees. Watch for the shielding effect while the ball is below the trees and the funnelling effect when it is above them. With a strong crosswind consider hitting a shot that will stay below the trees in order to take advantage of the shielding effect.
- Shutes. When hitting out of a shute watch for the shielding effect to stop when the ball passes the end of the trees.
- Terrain. When playing a sloping or rolling course with holes at different elevations, watch for all three effects.
- Buildings. If there are buildings near the course watch for the funnelling effect between them and the shielding affect in front.

The funnelling and shielding effects can result in a swirling wind. If you understand the causes of the swirling you may be able to determine the actual wind direction at your target area.

7.   GUSTING WINDS. Gusting refers to winds that change speed appreciably in a short period of time. These can be difficult to play in.

One way to handle them is to hit your shots coinciding with the gust of wind, either to the strong or the weak part of the gust. Time the gusts by counting to yourself as the speed changes and determine if the changes are consistent. If the gusts are not consistent then all you can do is make a guess and hit the shot.

However, if the gusts are consistently timed, you can take advantage of them. For example into a headwind, hit your shot when the gust is ending and with a tailwind, hit the shot when the gust is starting.

There is an unwritten rule regarding playing in these winds. It applies when you have a gusting crosswind and a bunker to the side of the green. In order to get the ball near the pin you have to start your ball over the bunker and let the wind blow it onto the green.

The unwritten rule is to avoid at all costs aiming a shot at a hazard. This is because almost every time you aim at a hazard, even though you may have timed the gusts perfectly, the moment your ball reaches the critical point, the wind will not gust.

I do not know why this is, I just know it has happened to me and others many times. Avoid aiming over a hazard. Accept being a little further away from the pin.

Chip shots and putts can also be affected by the wind, although not to the same extent. If a green is sheltered by trees there will probably be no effect. If a green is elevated and not shielded, or on very fast greens a strong wind can move a putt or chip shot. The ball is usually only affected in the last few feet (metres) as it slows down and it takes a strong wind to move the ball noticeably.

If the wind is strong enough to affect my balance while I am swinging, I adjust my body weight to lean into the wind. I am careful not to shift my weight too far because I do not want to fall over if the wind stops. This adjustment reduces the normal weight transfer during the swing resulting in a swing with less power so I use one club more.

Prior to a round in the wind I may change the makeup of my fourteen clubs. I may take out the 5 wood and replace it with my one iron. The one iron hits the ball lower and therefore the ball is easier to control in the wind. The problem is I must be in my best form to even have a chance of hitting the one iron well, so I rarely carry the club. Still I do own one and have used it occasionally.

Having a one iron in your bag is a status symbol. Hitting the club is another thing. Many people believe you are not "a player" unless you have a one iron. I have one but do not believe it makes me "a player". Well, at least not when I cannot hit it.

Playing well in the wind is a challenge. Once you learn how to adapt, it can also be fun. Well, at least interesting. Remember everyone's scores go up when playing in the wind.

SECTION 12.5 — CLOUDS AND BRIGHT SUNSHINE

Lighting conditions on a bright clear day are different than on a cloudy dull day. An improper adjustment for these differences can cost shots.

The amount of light shed on a course depends on the time of day, the type, height and amount of clouds and any shadows. The light affects two areas, on the greens and the judging of distances.

If the day is bright I can normally see the breaks on the green without looking too hard. Viewing the line from behind the ball and the low side is usually sufficient. The exception is when it is so bright and the angle of the sun is such that the light is reflected off the grass. This has the visual effect of flattening or smoothing out the rolls.

On a dull day I look at my putt from all angles, behind the ball, behind the hole and both sides of the line. The less light there is, the flatter the greens appear. This is apparent when you are playing the 18th green and it is almost totally dark. Unless it is very severe, a break cannot be seen.

On a dull day I accept my plumb bob technique as a better indication of the general roll than what I see with my eyes. Also on a dull day I am inclined to hit my putts a little firmer because I know I may not have noticed a subtle break, and a firmer putt will hold the line better.

The second area where the lighting can make a difference is in the judging of distances. Generally on a clear bright day objects tend to appear further away and on a dull day they appear closer. The effect the level of light has on the judging of distance is another reason I map out the yardages (metreages) of a course. I am not smart enough to figure out these and the other variables I have mentioned throughout this book to judge the distance by sight alone.

The lighting conditions on the course are just another of those small things that I am aware of and adjust to. In the long run little things like these add up to better scores.

CHAPTER 13
MAKING SHORT PUTTS

The ability to make short putts is the key to good scoring and the essence of "getting the ball in the hole". These are the scoring shots and must be treated as such. A mediocre drive can be recovered from, but a missed short putt is a shot gone forever.

Short putts, by my definition, are putts less than 6 feet (2 metres). With these putts I am deadly. In an average round I make at least 90 percent of my short putts at my home course.

To clarify, when I say I make 90 percent of my short putts I do not mean I make 90 percent of my 6 foot (2 metre) putts. I do mean that I make 90 percent that are less than 6 feet (2 metres). During a round most short putts are less than 4 feet (1 metre) and I make almost all of these. These are included in that figure.

I find most short putts are relatively easy. When compared to a full shot the mechanics are much slower and easier to execute. I believe it is within almost everyone's capability to be a good short putter. The exception is someone who has the yips. If you do — well, good luck.

As I have said before, when one cannot make short putts pressure is applied to every other area of the game. Knowing how to make short putts alleviates this pressure. The need to get every shot tight to the pin is no longer required.

The ability to make short putts will also dramatically increase the probability of the worst score on the hole being a bogey. For example, with a mediocre drive, as long as the ball is still in play, I can get the ball on or near the green (within wedge distance) in regulation strokes. From on or near the green, I can get the ball within 30 feet (9 metres) of the hole. From this distance I can get the ball within short putt range. From here I will make the putt.

To make a double bogey or worse requires more than one bad shot. Certainly a shot out of bounds or in the water will put you in danger of double bogey, but that is not keeping the ball in play.

A large part of the ability to make short putts is confidence. I have been able to reach a point where there simply is no doubt in my mind I will make the putt. On the rare occasions when I do miss a short putt, I immediately look for the real reason the putt was missed. I may blame a spike mark, footprint, bad greens or the manner in which the hole was cut. If I cannot find something to blame it on, I accept I have hit a bad putt and forget about it. I expect to hit a number of bad shots and do not let one bad shot bother me.

On the extremely extraordinary occasions where I hit a few bad putts I schedule a putting practice session. This session is described in Chapter 15 ROUTINES AND CHECKLISTS. At my current skill level I usually need only one practice session to get my putting back to the level I expect.

I learned how to make short putts by practising making short putts. Generally, I spent a couple of hours on the practice green experimenting to find a repeatable stroke and then adapted my technique around this repeatable stroke.

To start, I went out and hit 3 foot (1 metre) putts for an hour. I chose this distance because I could stroke the ball gently and watch the clubhead for the complete stroke. I experimented with everything I could think of, including:

- Grip. Placement of hands, overlap, Vardon, baseball, cross-handed, hands turned in one direction, forefinger down shaft, thumb positions.
- Stance. Upright or bent over, feet open, square or closed, weight distribution.
- Ball position. Forward or back in the stance and the distance the ball was away from my feet.
- Elbow and wrist. Varied the angles.
- Head position. Chin tucked in or not, head turned or not.

After I was satisfied the stroke looked and felt correct, I began to watch the ball to ensure it was going where I wanted it to. If I had any problems I made minor adjustments.

Although this sounds like a lot of work it was not. Many of the things I tried I rejected immediately. They just did not feel right.

When I started experimenting the only fundamentals I believed must be constant were to keep the shoulders square to the line and the wrists firm throughout the stroke. I had read these in a magazine article and they sounded good so I accepted them. Everything else about the putting stroke was subject to my own choice.

I also had a base to work from, my old natural putting stroke. My experimenting ended up changing only a few small things, my natural stroke was comfortable and a few changes made it repeatable.

Once I had my new stroke I noted where my feet were, how far bent over, ball position, grip, elbow angle, wrist angle, and initial clubhead backswing path.

I then practiced the setup and feel of the stroke in front of a full-length mirror. I checked that everything looked right and the clubhead was following the proper path. I was very careful to ensure the face of the putter remained square to the target line at the point of impact. I checked this by putting in slow motion.

Next, I had another practice session where I hit only 6 foot (2 metre) putts. I tried to make every one. This was the test of my stroke. I picked a flat spot on the green so I had a straight putt and hit every putt from the same spot. For each putt I was careful to setup in the precise manner I had decided was correct for me. I then watched the results.

When I was making the vast majority of the putts, I quit the session. I had my stroke for short putts. I had seen myself make a number of them and knew I could do the same on the course.

That is how I learned to make short putts. Just a few practice sessions where I experimented, setup properly for each practice putt and watched the results. If I had bad results I made an adjustment and tried again. Eventually I ended up with a comfortable repeatable stroke which I had confidence in.

This exercise also helped my longer putting. I figured if I could make short putts regularly I could make longer putts occasionally. I also knew I had a larger target area for my longer putts. This knowledge further improved my confidence and I became a better putter overall.

As a result of this exercise I came away with three main keys which I still use today. These are:

- Ball out. I play the ball further out from my body than most people. The ball is not directly under my eyes but a few inches (centimetres) away. I found during my practice session if I moved the ball closer I tended to take the club back to the outside and cut across every putt.
- Weight. At address I spread my weight evenly on both feet. This helps me remain steady during the stroke.
- Left elbow. I point my left elbow along the target line. This keeps the back stroke and forward stroke on the proper line, creating a feeling similar to a pendulum action.

It is absolutely essential I follow my putting routine for every putt. The routine is described in Chapter 15 ROUTINES AND CHECKLISTS. I suggest you review my routine, use it as a base and create your own. I am convinced a person will never be even a reasonable putter without some regular routine to follow.

A big factor in my ability to make short putts is the putting segment of my pre-round warmup routine. Prior to every round I refamiliarize myself with my putting stroke, check my alignment and mechanics are correct and get a feel for the speed of the greens. This warmup routine ensures I am putting correctly when I start a round and can therefore concentrate on reading the breaks and speed of the putts. I do not have to worry about the mechanics of the stroke when I am on the course.

I follow three general rules for short putts:

1. Make the putt. My only consideration is to get the ball in the hole. Three putting or laying up does not enter my mind. However if I have a slick downhill putt I am careful.
2. Work on the putt. A short tap-in can be handled quickly but from 2 feet (.7 metre) or more I ensure I spend the time and effort to line the putt up properly.
3. Not putt out. I rarely putt out after my first putt. If I proceed to hit the second putt immediately I tend to rush my routine. I also want a break to calm myself down. If I am not close to the hole I may be angry with myself over the way I hit my first putt. Letting someone else putt gives me time to gather my thoughts. I also do not want others to putt out because they may be standing in what may become the line for my next putt.

With short putts I choose my line from memory as often as I can. This is an important point. I do not have the skills to read greens well and putting from memory helps alleviate this. I suggest you do the same.

On my home course I make an effort to remember the breaks. I cannot remember them for every putt, but I try. I especially note a break if the ball does something I do not expect. Memorising the breaks on greens is a long term exercise, but over time one can become quite familiar with each green. Most greens are fairly consistent with only a few spots that have a different break.

Even knowing generally which way the green breaks helps by increasing the probability of my reading the specific putt correctly, and therefore increasing my probability of making the putt.

If you feel this is too much information to remember, you may want to keep a notebook and record the breaks. Divide the green into four sections and use arrows to indicate the direction. When on the course, as you are walking to the green have a quick look at your notes. In your notes you may also want to keep comments on the speed and amount of break. Some greens may be faster than others and the ball may break more.

When I have a conflict between what I remember and what I read on a putt, I usually go with what I remember. I have more confidence in my memory than my ability to read putts.

When I am on a strange course and have no memories of the greens I go through my normal reading routine. Generally, I look at the overall slope of the green and the length of the grass along with the direction of the grain (knapp). I also use the plumb-bob technique to determine the specific slope near the hole.

I concentrate most of my effort on the last 3 feet (1 metre) of the putt. This is where the putt will usually break the most because the slower the ball is moving the more susceptible it is to the rolls and slopes of the green. After that it becomes a gut feel as to what I think the break is. I make my decision and go with it.

I am still a very good short putter when I am on a strange course, I just do not make as many as I do on my home course. The biggest factor being again, memory.

I also have adjustments I make depending on the type of short putt:
1. Speed of the putt. If the green allows die-at-the-hole putting I remember to hit the putt softly. If the area around the hole is raised slightly I hit the putt a little firmer. The hole may be raised due to people stepping around it or being improperly cut by the greens staff.
2. Firm. If there is a small break and I am unsure of the direction I hit the putt a little firmer. This reduces the amount of break the putt will take.
3. Toe of putter. With a very fast downhill putt I may decide to hit the ball off the toe of the putter rather than the sweet spot. This reduces the chance of the putt going too far past the hole if hit too hard. The ball will be pushed slightly offline to the right so a proper adjustment is required.
4. Cutting. On very rare occasions I use a special technique of my own which involves intentionally cutting the putt to keep it on line. I use this technique only when I have real doubts as to the amount of break because it is difficult to execute. I use it only on right to left putts from 2 to 9 feet (1 to 3 metres) in length. I developed this technique because of problems I had on one green at my home course.

The technique involves opening the face of the putter about 10 degrees and changing the path of the putter to slightly out to in, across the ball. This imparts sidespin and for a right to left putt the ball will be spinning slightly against the break and will run straighter. I aim just inside the right lip and hit the putt firm. This gives me a wider margin for error with the speed and break of the putt.

This is a useful technique to have in your skill set but must be practised to be used properly. It also requires one to have a lot of confidence in their putting ability. If you do not have the confidence do not play with fancy issues like this, it can ruin your regular putting stroke.

5.   Aiming point. On short putts I do not aim at the center of the hole. I aim one inch (2.5 centimetres) left of the exact center. I have a tendency to hit my putts slightly to the right of my target and aiming to the left allows me to use the complete width of the hole.

I have had many putts fall in the right side that would not have gone in had I aimed at the center of the hole. Find out what your tendency is and allow for it.

If you miss regularly on both sides, try forcing a tendency by adjusting the ball position in your stance. Moving the ball back in your stance will force a tendency to hit putts to the right. Moving the ball forward will force a tendency to hit putts left. Usually only a small adjustment is required. Choose the one you feel most comfortable with.

6.   Adjustment for glasses. This is discussed in Chapter 10 EQUIP-MENT Section GLASSES, but generally I have to be careful when I am standing over a short putt to ignore the location of the hole as I see it from the corner of my eye. The location where the hole appears to be is not where the hole actually is. This is an optical illusion caused by the curvature of the lenses. I adjust by concentrating on putting the ball over a mark on the green just in front of the ball.

Every so often, spend a few minutes practising 3 foot (1 metre) putts to get used to seeing the ball go into the hole. This helps build confidence in your short putt stroke.

In summary, the ability to make short putts is extremely important. If you can make short putts you reduce the pressure on every other area of your game.

Experiment to learn a consistent repeatable stroke. Once you have this stroke maintain your confidence level by looking for the real reason putts are missed.

Work hard on every putt and make an effort to memorize (or make notes of) the breaks on the greens at your home course. Prior to every round refamiliarize yourself with your putting stroke and check your alignment and mechanics are correct.

The ability to make short putts is the key to getting the ball in the hole. Getting the ball in the hole is the key to the whole game.

CHAPTER 14
PROBLEM DIAGNOSIS

This chapter lists the recurring mechanical problems I have with my golf game and includes the remedies which correct them. I include these problems and remedies to provide examples and show how simple the remedies are.

The same errors creep into my game regularly and when I am having problems these are the first things I look for. If the symptoms of a problem appear similar to one of my recurring problems, I try one of my remedies.

These lists are presented as examples of what may be a cause of a problem. Any one fault or a combination of several faults may be the cause of a specific problem. The faults listed here are the most frequent faults which occur for me. I have learned to identify these faults and determined the appropriate remedies over the years.

SECTION 14.1 — FULL SWING PROBLEMS
1. Slicing or weak pop up shots. Usually the result of an alignment error with the ball too far forward. The remedy is to correct alignment. Another possible cause is not finishing the backswing, or in other words starting my downswing before completing the backswing. This ruins my timing. The remedy is to concentrate on hesitating at the top of the backswing.
2. Consistently hitting slots thin. Usually due to lifting my head, especially when I am anxious about the result of the shot. The remedy is to create a swing key that forces me to keep my head down until I am well through the ball. I do not worry about watching where the ball goes because my playing partners will do that if it is a bad shot. If it is a good shot I will know where it is.
3. Shots not travelling as far as usual. First I wonder about the humidity and whether the air is exceptionally dense (see Chapter 12 WEATHER FACTORS). If this is not the cause then I am usually just not swinging hard enough or quitting on the downswing. Remedy is to create a swing key that forces me to accelerate through the ball.
4. Hitting shots fat (behind the ball). Usually due to my not starting the downswing with my legs resulting in poor timing. The remedy is to concentrate on my usual swing keys of hesitating at the top of my backswing and starting the downswing with my legs. Another possible cause is quitting on the downswing or not swinging hard enough. Remedies for both these problems are discussed in the previous point.

119

5. Pushing shots. This is frequently due to an alignment error where I have the ball too far back in my stance. Remedy is to correct alignment. I have to be careful here in what may appear to be a push may in fact be due to cutting across the ball very sharply. I check the direction of the divot to determine the cause. The remedy is to concentrate on my normal swing key of starting with my legs which reduces the chance of cutting across the ball.

6. Spraying shots, one left one right or no control over the direction. This is usually due my tempo being off by my not finishing the backswing. May also be an alignment problem where for some reason I am not setting up to the target properly and am making some compensation during the swing. Remedy is to check alignment when I have a spare moment and to ensure I am finishing my backswing.

    This could also be due to my shifting my weight on the backswing to the outside of my right foot. When I do this I usually do not get the weight back to the left side in time. Remedy is move the toe of my right (back) foot slightly to the right (open).

7. No results from the above quick remedies. If I still cannot diagnose or fix the problem I go back to basics. When I have a moment between shots I check the following:
    *   Grip. Hands in correct position.
    *   Alignment. I check I am aiming properly. This involves picking a spot on the ground as for a normal shot and lining up to it. I then place the shaft of a club across my shoulders and move away still holding the club in place. The shaft should be pointing on a line parallel to the target line. I do the same check with my hips and feet. In the case of my feet I lay the club on the ground in front of my toes. If there is a fault my remedy is to ensure that whatever was misaligned is correct for the remainder of the round.

8. Desperate. If nothing has worked so far I may invent something new to try or assume I am having a bad day and not worry about it. Forgetting about the problem sometimes, although rarely, fixes the problem.

SECTION 14.2 — WEDGE AND CHIPPING PROBLEMS

1. Hitting shots thin. This is almost always due to lifting my head because I am anxious to see the results of the shot. Easy remedy, concentrate on keeping my head down.
2. Hitting shots fat. Usually due to setting up with my weight on the right side rather than the left.

3. Shanks. I occasionally have this problem with partial wedge shots due I believe, to a flaw in my swing where I tend to cut across the ball. The remedy is to remember to line up with the ball closer to the toe of the club. I accept this as a problem and am not willing to change my swing to correct it.

SECTION 14.3 — PUTTING PROBLEMS

1. Pushing and pulling putts. Almost always an address problem. I am either positioning the ball too far forward or back in my stance. The remedy is to double check the ball placement before actually making the putting stroke.
2. Hitting the ground before the ball. Usually due to having the ball forward in my stance. It can also be caused by an uneven surface behind the ball. Or it may indicate I am breaking my wrists during the putting stroke.

    On long putts, this is a symptom I am dipping my body during the stroke. I do not know why I do it and the only way I can stop it is by concentrating on not dipping my head during the putting stroke. This remedy does not work all the time. If it does not, I just wait for the problem to go away and eventually it does.
3. Hitting putts thin. Occasionally this results from having the ball too far back in the stance, but more often it is from lifting my head or moving my body during the putting stroke. The quick fix is to keep my head down and ensure I do not move my body until I have finished the stroke.
4. Having trouble getting the feel of the speed of the greens or hitting one putt long and the next one short. This is a tough problem to correct. Possible causes are inconsistent contact on the putterhead, greens not being cut resulting in uneven growth and thus a variance in the speed of the green, the yips, incorrect reading of the slope or grain (knapp), an inconsistent green surface or the golf gods disliking me that day.

    The remedy is to keep trying. A helpful hint is to pace off the length of each putt and adjust the number based on the terrain.

These are the recurring problems which creep into my game. Keep track of the problems you have and the remedies that work for you. Watch for the problems when you are on the course and try the remedy you feel is appropriate at the time. By correctly identifying problems and implementing the proper remedy you may be able to turn a bad round into a mediocre round or even save a good score.

75 Occasionally

CHAPTER 15
ROUTINES AND CHECKLISTS

This chapter covers the routines and checklists I use. They have been developed over many years and are as comprehensive as I can make them. I suggest you review them and select the appropriate points to create your own.

The FULL AND PARTIAL SHOT and PUTTING routines assist me in preparing for a shot. They help me focus my concentration, ensure I set up properly and reduce the chance of my forgetting to consider all the factors necessary to get a ball to the intended target. In short, these routines increase my consistency. I have memorized them and ensure I complete them prior to every shot. I believe they are a major contributing factor to my reaching the level of skill I have.

SECTION 15.1 — FULL AND PARTIAL SHOT ROUTINE
My full shot routine is:
1.   I start my routine as I am approaching the tee or the ball. My first step is to review any shot I can remember of a similar nature. If I am approaching a tee I think of how I have played the hole in the past, including which clubs I have used and the aiming point.

If I am approaching a shot from the fairway or rough I recall the clubs I used from a similar distance and the results I have achieved. For example I may have regularly dumped a shot into a bunker, or missed the green left, or gone over the back of the green. I also try to remember how the terrain of the green will affect the ball after it lands. There may be a severe slope or soft spots or firm spots.
2.   I then look at the pin position (left or right) and consider the flight path needed to get near the pin. If I am on a par 5 and not approaching the green, I pick a general target area that will give me the best approach for the next shot.
3.   Next, I consider the wind direction and strength, the temperature and humidity and how I am hitting the ball that day. Some days I hit the ball well and other days weak. If it is early in the round I assume my average club distances adjusted for the weather conditions. As I play I make further adjustments based on the results I am achieving that day. This results in a WEATHER AND CURRENT FORM ADJUSTMENT FACTOR which I calculate and store in my head.
4.   I calculate the distance of the shot if I am less than 240 yards (215 meters) from the pin. This is critical. If I am playing a course I have

mapped, I know the distance to the middle of the green from a landmark. I pace off the distance from the landmark to my ball and then allow for the pin position.

Generally, if the pin is at the back of the green I add 10 yards (9 metres) to the shot and if the pin is at the front I subtract 10 yards (9 metres). If the pin is around the middle I adjust the yardage (metreage) based on what looks right. Touring professionals are given maps of the pin placements prior to a round showing how far a pin is from the front of the green and from the edge, so they can be very accurate. Without the luxury of maps we amateurs have to learn to estimate distances to the pin positions. My method of working from the middle of the green is fairly accurate. I would love to have exact distances as I am sure on a good day it would save me a shot or two. Only on a good day though.

I apply my WEATHER AND CURRENT FORM ADJUSTMENT FACTOR to this distance, giving me a PLAYING DISTANCE.

5. I then assess the lie of the ball and determine a LIE FACTOR comprised of a LEVEL LIE FACTOR and a GRASS LIE FACTOR. The LEVEL LIE FACTOR includes whether the lie is uphill, downhill, sidehill or flat. The GRASS LIE FACTOR includes examining how the ball is sitting in the grass. Is the ball on a bare lie (sitting on dirt), fluffy (some grass likely to come between the ball and the clubface), in light rough (2 inches (5 centimetres) or less and the ball sitting up) or in heavy rough (down in more than 2 inches (5 centimetres) of grass). A perfect lie is where the ball is not above or below your feet (level) and is sitting on top of approximately half an inch (1.3 centimetres) of grass.

I calculate a LIE FACTOR based on these two components and the type of shot I am going to play. The LIE FACTOR is composed of the LEVEL LIE FACTOR and the GRASS LIE FACTOR adjusted for each other.

If the lie is perfect I ignore the LIE FACTOR and use the PLAYING DISTANCE calculated in the step above for club selection and go to the next step of the routine.

If the lie is not perfect I apply the LIE FACTOR to the PLAYING DISTANCE for club selection. This is not a simple calculation and one factor can override the other depending on the situation. I will summarise the issues here by giving examples:

- If I have a uphill, downhill or sidehill lie, I add one club (take a 6 iron not a 7) to what I would normally hit from that PLAYING DISTANCE. If the lie is severe I add two clubs unless this forces me to a long iron, where I would probably hit an easy 5 wood.

Hitting long irons off severe or difficult lies is beyond my ability.
I also think it is beyond everyone except the most accomplished
players.

- If the ball is sitting down in heavy rough I never hit a 3 or 4 wood
or a long iron. In extreme cases the lie may be so bad I am forced
to hit a wedge just to get the ball out. For distance I use a 5 wood.
- If the ball is in light rough or a fluffy lie I usually subtract a club
(7 iron instead of 6) because the ball will run more than normal.
If there is a bunker to carry, I do not subtract the club but hit the
club I need to carry the bunker.
- If the ball is on a bare lie I use the normal club and play it slightly
back in my stance.

If I am in doubt I take one more club and swing easy. I must have
a high level of confidence in my ability to execute the shot correctly
before I will play it. This helps keep my confidence at a high level. I try
not to set myself up for failure by trying extremely difficult and impossible
shots.

6.   I mentally select the proper club and decide whether to hit the shot
hard, normal or soft.

7.   I now remind myself of the swing keys I want to use during this shot.
Possible swing keys are discussed in another section of this chapter.

8.   After all the above I am still not ready to address the ball. I take the
club out of the bag and if on the tee choose a spot to tee off from.

On the tee I first choose a side of the tee box depending on my target
area. At this time I have not yet chosen my specific target area, but I do
have a general idea of where it will be. If the target area is to the left I hit
from the right side of the tee. If the target area is to the right I hit from the
left side. The exceptions are when there is a strong crosswind or I plan
to hook or slice the ball.

When choosing a spot within the teeing ground I avoid a severe
downhill, uphill or sidehill lie. I try to find a level spot.

You may want to vary this sometimes if you are planning to hit a
curved shot or want to reduce the chance of hitting an unintentional slice
or hook. If you are trying to hit a hook, or trying to reduce a slice, choose
a spot that is slightly uphill and where the ball is above your feet. If you
are trying to hit a slice or reduce a hook, choose a spot that puts the ball
slightly below your feet. I avoid downhill lies whenever I can because I
find them too hard to play.

Only use slight variations in the slope, severe ones increase the
difficulty of the shot too much.

9.   Next I choose a specific target area and a line to aim along. I consider the wind, any hazards, interceding trees or anything within a reasonable margin for error on both sides of my chosen line.

10. I then choose a mark on the ground on my target line approximately 1 foot (.3 of a metre) in front of the ball. I use this mark to align to the target during address. I am careful to choose this mark from directly behind the ball and make doubly sure that the mark is on the line I want. A small error here can mean an excellent shot ending up in trouble.

In the case of a drive that will go 200 yards (180 meters) or more, an error of an inch (a couple of centimeters) in choosing the alignment mark will result in a shot hit perfectly down the erroneous target line being off by at least 20 yards (18 meters). If your shot is slightly offline, which happens frequently to me, an alignment error can make the difference between being on the fairway and being stymied behind a tree. Errors like this add shots to your score.

I am so fussy about choosing my aiming point that I follow a special procedure to ensure I get the spot correct. This procedure is designed to compensate for any distortion caused by the curvature of the lenses on my glasses. The steps in this routine are:

- I stand directly behind the ball and face my target.
- I bring my right hand up in front of my eyes, keeping the fingers straight and pointing vertically. With my hand in line with the target, the pin for example, I line up my eyes in the center of the lenses of my glasses. This gives the appearance of the fingers being directly in line with my target.
- The next step is the important one. I move my hand straight down until the line intersects the ground a foot (.3 of a metre) in front of my ball. I take care to bring my hand down in a perfectly vertical line, countering a natural tendency to veer towards the right.
- The point where my hand intersects the ground is the point that is perfectly in line with my target. I then find a blemish or discoloration in the grass to use as my alignment point. I am as precise as possible in choosing this mark.

10a. This is the point in the routine where some people visualize the shot. They mentally create a picture of the anticipated flight of the ball. Many professionals recommend this be done. I do not do this for full shots because it does not seem to add anything to the shot for me. I do something similar for putts. I mention it here for information only, that is why the point number is 10a.

11. I am now ready to address the ball. As I step away from behind the ball I tug my shirt on my left shoulder. This ensures the shirt is not too tight and does not restrict my swing. This ritual has also become a superstition.

12. I place the club lightly behind the ball without taking a formal stance. I then pull the club away, step away from the ball, and take an easy practice swing.

This practice swing is usually not designed to rehearse the shot but to get the general feel of the club I am going to use and the angle I must maintain for my hands and body. These angles vary from club to club and I like to get the feel of them before I hit the shot. A driver requires a more upright body and a different angle with the wrists than a wedge.

I would not argue with anyone taking a full practice swing before every shot. There is a benefit in rehearsing a shot. Please only one or two practice swings. Anymore can annoy other players.

In three situations I will take complete practice swings:
- When I have a non-level lie. To get the feel of the shot.
- When I am hitting out of light or heavy rough. Longer grass can impede the clubface and even force it closed. A practice swing helps me gauge the amount of resistance and to see if the clubface is going to be twisted. If there is a lot of resistance I take more club. If I think the clubface is going to be closed I aim a little further right and firm up my grip. I may also decide to hit the ball from a steeper angle. Iron clubs are affected by this closing of the clubface more than woods.
- Short or partial wedge shots. I like to get the feel of a partial shot before I hit the shot. In this case I rehearse the force of the swing.

13. I place the clubface behind the ball and check it is square to my aiming mark on the ground.

14. I position my feet one foot at a time. I make a quick visual check to ensure my feet are square to the line. If I am trying to hook or slice my feet will be closed or open as needed.

15. Check my grip on the club. I do this by feel.

16. I may or may not look at the target (the pin). Sometimes, for reasons I do not know, when I look at the target I feel I am improperly aligned. This frequently occurs when the tee or surrounding trees are not on the same line as my target line. My general rule is from the fairway I take a quick peak at the target, but from the tee I do not.

17. I check the ball position in my stance. I do not hit every shot off the left heel. I play my driver off the left heel but as I move through the other

clubs I gradually move the ball back. For a wedge shot the ball is almost off my right (rear) heel. For my 5 iron the ball is near the middle of my stance. This is one of those issues that each player has to experiment with and determine what works best for them.

18. I check my weight distribution. I do this by shifting my weight from foot to foot until I am comfortable. I want my weight to be evenly distributed with a slight favoring to the insides of both feet. I also like my weight to be slightly back on my heels at the start of the swing. I have a tendency to fall forward on my shots especially when I am trying to hit it long.

19. I waggle the clubhead a couple of times.

20. Next I again visually check my clubface is still properly aligned with the aiming spot on the ground.

21. I firm up my left elbow. Just a slight tensing of my left arm to make sure it is not too loose.

22. If all is okay I remind myself of the swing keys I want to use. My swing keys vary depending on the shot. My usual swing keys are; take club back slowly, hesitate at top and begin forward swing with legs. I also remind myself of the force I want to hit the shot (hard, normal or soft).

23. GO.

To a person who does not have a similar routine, what I have just described will probably seem mind boggling. In actual fact it is not. With repetition these routines become second nature.

They have become so familiar to me I can go through the total address sequence in a few seconds. The visual checks only take a glance, things either look right or they do not. From point 11 to GO takes approximately 8 seconds. I go through as many items as possible while I am waiting for my turn to play.

You should always be conscious of slow play. If you spend too much time on these routines you will hold up others in your group. They may decide to harass you about it and that can affect your concentration.

SECTION 15.2 — SWING KEYS

The stages of the swing as I see it, along with possible swing keys for each stage are:

1. Takeaway:
    - Take club back slowly.
    - Keep club low to the ground.
    - Turn hips in.
    - Pick club up steeply (for special shots).

2. Top of backswing:
   - Stop or hesitate at top.
   - Wait for lower body to coil (feel tension).
   - Adjust club position higher or lower.
   - Check weight on inside of right foot, not outside.
   - Check wrists are cocked.
   - Check direction shaft is pointing.
3. Start of downswing, first thought when beginning forward motion:
   - Begin with legs, lateral movement of left knee.
   - Begin with arms.
   - Slice or hook the ball (when I am intentionally trying to curve the ball I think "hook" or "slice").
4. Forward motion of club:
   - Accelerate through the ball.
   - Wait for clubhead.
   - Release wrists late.
   - Chop down into ball (special shots).
   - Actively release wrists (for high flip wedge shots).
   - Wrists firm (for putting and chipping).
   - Head down.
5. Throughout swing:
   If I am working on improving my tempo I count to myself as I swing. I vary the speed of each stage based on the count. For example with a slow backswing, hesitate at top and normal forward swing, I would think "Zeee-roo, one, two." I extend the zero to ensure I am slow in that stage.

At any one time the maximum I use is one swing key for each stage of the swing. This is all I can mentally handle. The specific keys I use vary depending on the current shot situation and any problems I may be having.

Using swing keys helps me focus on the execution of the swing and increases the probability of my hitting a good shot.

SECTION 15.3 — PUTTING ROUTINE
I begin my PUTTING ROUTINE as I am walking towards the green. As soon as I see where the ball is in relation to the pin I start thinking about my putt.
1. First, I try to remember if I have encountered a similar putt in the past. If so, I think about the break and speed of the previous putt.

2.   I go to my ball and mark it. For a putt of 15 feet (5 metres) or more I use a tee to mark the ball unless it is near someone else's line. A tee is easier to see from other parts of the green, with swales a ball marker or coin can be difficult to discern. For short putts I use a ball marker so there is no distraction for other players.

I set aside a special tee for this purpose and keep it in a separate pocket from my other tees. If I have a good round I continue to use it until I think the luck has worn off.

3.   Clean the ball. Be careful how you clean your ball. Most courses use chemicals that can be dangerous to your health. I heard a story a few years ago about a fellow who developed a rare lung fungus from licking his golf ball.

4.   Next I think about the overall slope of the green. Does it slope from right to left, vice versa, front to back or back to front (the most common). I need to determine how the green sits in relation to the true center of gravity. This can be misleading, since the overall terrain may be sloped in one direction while the green is flat or sloped in another direction.

To determine the true center of gravity I look at other factors. I mentioned my home course is in a river valley. The river is much smaller than it was 100,000 years ago but it is an indication of the terrain. After analyzing where water flows on the course after a heavy rain I came to the logical conclusion that the terrain generally slopes towards the existing river. Therefore putts will generally break towards the river. The old golfing adage "All putts break towards water" is worth remembering.

The problem with this adage is it is not true in all cases. The slope of the green will override this, as will different types of grass, some grasses follow the setting sun. Find out what applies at your course and remember it.

5.   The next step is setting a default speed for reading the putt. When looking at a putt, my first concern is direction, I usually do not decide on the exact speed of the putt until I am over the ball. As the direction is of course dependent on the speed, because a firmly hit putt will break less, I assume a speed that will take the ball between 6 inches (15 centimetres) and 1 foot (30 centimetres) beyond the hole.

There are two exceptions to using this default speed. The first, is some greens allow die-at-the-hole putting. Personally I prefer this because the hole is a little larger. A slow moving ball that just catches the edge of the hole will probably drop. A putt moving at a faster speed will spin out or go over the edge.

The second exception is when the ball will break away from the hole if the putt is too slow. There are to two possible causes for this. The first is the depression caused by people stepping near the hole to remove their ball. This has the effect of raising the hole slightly. The second is due to the hole being cut incorrectly. If the greenskeeper is not careful when he or she cuts the hole the result can be a raised area around the hole.

The speed required to keep the ball on line depends upon the severity of the raised area. It will definitely be firmer than the speed for the die-at-the-hole situation. So adjust accordingly. The amount the area is raised also depends on the time of day. Late in the day the hole is more likely to be raised. If a course gets a lot of play this can be significant.

6.   If playing a course where the grain (knapp) is a factor I walk to the hole and examine the length of the grass and the direction of the grain. The grain goes in the direction from the edge with grass overhanging it to the edge that is bare. The amount the grain will affect the break of the putt depends on the length and type of grass and the amount of moisture on the green. The only way I know to learn how to judge the effect is to play and watch the differences in all conditions.

7.   I replace my ball on the green and remove my ball marker.

8.   Next I get directly behind the ball, squat and look at the line from the ball to the hole. If the slope is not severe I concentrate on the 3 feet (1 metre) from the hole. This is where most of the break will occur.

I also use the plumb-bob technique to determine the direction of the break. The plumb-bob technique is where you hold the putter at the top of the grip with the thumb and forefinger, letting it dangle freely. Keep the blade of the putter pointing towards you or directly away to overcome any distortion caused by the weight of the putterhead. Line the shaft up with the ball.

The position of the hole in relation to the shaft is the direction of the break. If the hole is to the left of the shaft the putt will break to the left. The amount of break is dependent on this and the other factors (like grain) mentioned in this section.

If the putt will have more than one break the plumb-bob technique will indicate the overall direction of the break. I then have to determine a separate break for each segment of the putt. When analysing the break remember the early portions will not have as much break as the later portions because the ball is moving faster in the early portions.

9.   Once I have a general idea of the breaks involved with the putt, I look at the line from the side to confirm what I have seen is true. I check that

the high side of the rolls are actually higher than the surrounding terrain. Looking at the putt from the side also gives me a feel for the distance of the putt. This is a better perspective than behind the ball.

If my memory of similar putts and what I have seen so far agree, I am convinced I have the break figured out correctly. I look at the putt from behind the hole only if I am not sure of the break or if the light is poor.

10. With the above information and based on past experience I now choose the line for the putt.

11. I select a spot as my alignment mark to putt over. I prefer the mark to be between 4 and 10 inches (10 to 25 centimetres) in front of the ball for putting. If I have trouble finding a mark I stare at the chosen spot until I have my clubface aligned properly.

12. I am now ready to address the putt. As I step away from behind the ball I tug my shirt on my left shoulder. This is a habit I have for full shots and I also do it for putts.

13. Next I grip the putter and step near the ball. I take a couple of practice swings just to get the feel of the putting stroke.

14. I place the clubface behind the ball taking care that the clubface is square to my alignment mark.

15. I take my stance and make a quick visual check to ensure my feet are square to the line. If I am currently using an open stance for putting, which I do quite often, I check the feet are open.

16. I check the ball position.

17. I check my weight distribution.

18. I look at the line I have chosen, following the complete line from the ball to the hole with my eyes. This is a form of visualization that also serves as a quick check to confirm my chosen line and speed seem right.

19. I now think only of the speed of the putt. I concentrate on the distance to the hole and allow my mind to "see" the length and path of the putt. I let my body and brain naturally choose the force of the stroke. I do not consciously program or choose the force required or even the length of the stroke. I just let it happen.

20. I visually check the clubface is still properly aligned with my aiming spot.

21. I remind myself of my swing keys, which are:
- Easy smooth stroke.
- Take the club back slowly.
- Accelerate through the ball.

22. GO. If all is well I hit the putt. If all is very well the putt goes in.

Those are the steps for my complete putting routine. Develop a routine of your own and remember to follow it for every putt.

Following are general comments on putting.

A straight uphill putt is relatively easy. Watch for things like footprints and spike marks. Such a putt can be hit firm because the back of the cup is higher than the front of the hole and will act as a backstop.

With a very fast downhill breaking putt on a bumpy green, I simply hit the putt and hope for the best. A putt such as this is at the mercy of the terrain around the hole, and can be easily deflected. If I miss one of these putts I do not worry about it.

Sidehill putts require not only the correct direction but also the correct speed. There is less margin for error on these putts. Remember when playing a sidehill putt the door to the hole is not the side of the hole facing you directly, but the side where the ball will approach the hole.

I have occasionally had rounds where I could visualize the line of the putt and the ball going in the hole. It was almost like having a line on the green indicating where the putt should go. If this has happened to you, you understand, if not, it cannot be explained. Whenever this happens I putt great. Unfortunately, I can not bring this feeling about. It just comes. It is also rare. I have no explanation or even a guess as to why it happens or under what conditions it occurs.

A lot of strokes can be saved by good putting so I recommend you find someone to teach you how to read greens properly. I did not realise how ignorant I was in this area until recently.

When faced with a greenside chip shot I treat the chip like a long putt. I read the green and although not expecting to chip the ball into the hole, I do play the shot to make it. If you do not try to make the chip shot you never will, but if you do try, occasionally one will go in. Chip shots tend not to break as much as putts. I do not know why.

I remember hearing two stories from an English friend of mine who watched Jack Nicklaus, David Graham and Tom Weiskopf play a practice round for the British Open. The first story, which does not relate to putting but I found interesting, occurred on a long par 4. Jack Nicklaus had driven into a fairway bunker with a steep face, approximately 180 yards (165 metres) from the green. Because of the steep face Jack needed an 8 iron to clear it.

My friend was standing about 40 yards (35 metres) away from Jack when he made a comment to his mate that Jack would never make it to the green. Well, Jack put the ball on the middle of the green about 20 feet (6 metres) from the hole.

My friend and his mate walked up to the green to watch them putt. Jack carefully lined up his putt and made it for what my friend thought was an incredible birdie. Jack then went to the hole, picked out the ball and walked over to my friend. Jack handed him the ball and said with a smile "You thought I couldn't get on the green?"

My friend was so flabbergasted he could not think of anything to say other than "Great shot". For verification of his story I asked him to show me the ball. Sure enough, the next time I saw him he showed me a ball that had Jack Nicklaus' name on it and no manufacturers label. When I heard this story I became a fan of Jack's, and I am not a fan of many people.

The second story, which does relate to putting dealt with how Jack, David Graham and Tom Weiskopf prepared for the tournament. When they got to the greens they ignored the pin placement and each went to a separate spot on the green.

They then putted to their chosen spot. They hit a number of putts from all directions and watched the breaks carefully. After a couple of minutes they rotated positions. When I asked my friend about this he thought they were putting to the spots where the pins would be placed during the tournament.

Hearing this story made me wonder how good the professionals are at reading greens. Perhaps they do it from memory most of the time also. Good stories.

A comment about spike marks. The rules do not allow for the situation where there have been a hundred hackers on a green who do not know how to walk in golf shoes and never repair spike marks. It can be incredible sometimes. The Etiquette section in the rules states each player should repair spike marks before they leave the green. Please do so.

SECTION 15.4 — PRE-ROUND WARMUP ROUTINE

I require at least 20 minutes to go through my warmup routine prior to a round. I need this time to get into the correct mental state, loosen my muscles and refamiliarize myself with my swing, putting stroke and chipping touch.

I start the routine as I approach the practice putting green. While I am walking I make a conscious effort to slow down my thinking. I may be in one of my hyper moods where my mind is racing. This happens to me occasionally, especially when I am late or have a lot of things to do.

My routine is as follows:

1.   The initial step is to begin to loosen the muscles. I take my sand wedge and swing the club in a circular motion over and around my head. This loosens up the shoulders. I make ten swings with each arm.

2.   I then take ten slow practice swings, still with the sand wedge. On the first swing I take the club back to about three quarters and then gradually lengthen each swing so that by the tenth swing I am taking the club back to parallel.

3.   I select my 5 wood and put a weighted doughnut on it. I use the 5 wood because I like the feel of the swing with this length of club. I take five and only five full swings with this weighted club. The first swing is fairly easy and by the third swing I am swinging full but not hard. I take only five swings because more stretches my muscles too much and they will be sore later in the round.

4.   Next I pull out my putter and three golf balls. I now proceed to go through my putting warm up routine, which consists of the following:

- I place the three balls approximately 10 feet (3 metres) from the hole. The hole I choose does not matter at this time.
- I take a couple of practice swings just to get the feel of the stroke.
- I line up and hit the first three putts quickly. If I miss it does not matter, I am just getting the feel of hitting putts again. I may repeat this exercise three or four times until it feels right. "Feels right" is hard to define. I need to sense my stroke is smooth and I am making good contact. Another indicator is the ball should not skid or bounce.

5.   Once I feel comfortable with my putting stroke I check my setup. I take my stance over the ball and go through my checklist:

- Check the grip. Normally I do this by feel, but if I have been having problems with my putting I visually check the position of my hands. I frequently experiment with my grip by changing thumb positions and turning one or both hands in either direction.
- Then my feet. Sometimes I putt with my feet square to the line and sometimes I open the stance (move the front foot back a bit). I choose the stance that feels right at the time.
- Next I visually check the ball is in the proper position in my stance. This check is important because I have a tendency to let the ball creep forward if I am not careful. Many people play their putts with the ball off their left heel. I play mine about 3 inches (7 centimetres) back from my left heel.

- I check my weight distribution, how far bent over I am and the angles of my elbows and wrists.
- The last step is a check on the alignment of the clubface. Is it square to the target or slightly open or closed. Depending on the make of putter I am using I have a tendency to incorrectly align the clubface in both directions. I tend to align my Ping with the face open and the Zebra with the face closed. Why I misalign these clubs is due to the way the clubface appears to me when I am over the ball. I suspect it may also have something to do with my wearing glasses.

The putting checklist is now complete. For people who do not play regularly, familiarisation routines such as this can be very important. If you have not done something for awhile the body and brain forget.

6.   I now find a hole without any break. I line up and putt three balls from 3 feet (1 metre). I putt all the balls from the same spot. I am trying to have every ball go into the hole at the very center. After I have hit the three putts I look at the results. If all three have gone in the center of the hole and everything feels right I go to the next step.

If I have pulled or pushed the putts I make corrections and hit another three putts. I continue this sequence until I get it right. If I am not confident I can make a three foot (1 metre) putt on the golf course I know I will play badly. I will not go to the next step until I have fixed any problem I have. If this takes all my warmup time I accept it and go to the tee. I will continue to make corrections on the course until I know I am putting properly.

7.   I am now confident I am putting the ball correctly and my stroke is in reasonable shape. My next step is practising short breaking putts. I look for a hole cut on a knoll and with a break of about one or two inches (3 to 5 centimetres) from 3 feet (1 metre).

I hit putts from both sides of the hole to ensure I can handle breaks in both directions. I do not try to make these putts but try to have the ball go over a specific corner of the cup. Setting my target as small as possible forces me to be very accurate. I usually hit two or three groups of putts from both sides.

8.   The next step in my pre-round warmup routine is hitting a few putts from gradually longer distances. I will hit about three to four more groups of the three balls from about 5 feet (2 metres) to 12 feet (4 metres). These distances are approximate, I do not measure them.

I try to make these putts but do not worry if they do not go in. I am mainly trying to groove my stroke and get a feel for the force I must use for varying distances. I also hit these putts quickly without going through my putting checklist.

There are two things to watch for here regarding speed of the greens. First, watch for slopes on the practice green and allow for them. If I continuously practice uphill putts I have a tendency to hit all my putts too hard for the first few holes. The same goes for downhill putts except I will tend to hit the putts short.

The second point is the speed of the practice green is often quite different from the speed of the greens on the course. If you are at your home course you should know how much difference there is and adjust. If you are on a strange course ask people who play there regularly, or the person in the pro shop.

If I know a practice green is faster or slower than the greens on the course, I go through a speed adjustment routine. This routine involves hitting three groups of three balls from about 10 feet (3 metres). When hitting these putts I do not think about the stroke or alignment, but concentrate on how hard I hit the putt.

For cases where the practice green is faster than the greens on the course, I try to hit the putts past the hole. My target distance past the hole depends on the amount of difference between the practice green and course greens. When I am not sure I use 2 feet (70 centimetres), or 20 percent, as an arbitrary distance. If the practice green is slower than the course greens I intentionally hit the putts short.

This speed adjustment routine I believe, improves my gauging of the speed of the putts on the course. If my putts are 20 percent short or long on the first few holes this may cost me shots, especially if I have a number of long putts early in the round. Also if I three putt the first two greens I am not happy and it can bother me.

9. I now hit two or three groups of 30 to 40 foot (9 to 12 metre) putts to get the feel of making a longer stroke with the putter. It also gives me more information on the general speed of the green, but I do not concentrate on the speed, just the mechanics and feel of the stroke for long putts.

This completes the putting portion of my warmup routine. I then begin the chipping segment.

10. The purpose of the chipping routine is to get the feel of my chipping stroke and regain my short game touch. I use my sand wedge because I hit the highest and the shortest chip shots with this club.

137

The first three or four groups of chip shots will be to about 15 to 20 feet (5 to 6 metres). There are no checklists here, I just try to make good contact and get the ball airborne without scooping during the stroke.

For the second segment I try to hit the ball as short a distance as possible while still making good contact. These chips may only fly a couple of feet before they land. I continue to hit these shots until I am comfortable with the results.

For me to hit a chip which lands 2 feet (.7 metres) away requires a deliberate and controlled swing. If I am not calm I cannot make this shot. The nerves take over and I tend to accelerate through the ball too fast resulting in the ball being hit too hard. This is the shot that requires the most "touch" from me. I am trying to regain this touch from the last time I played. This completes my chipping segment.

11. The next step is to take out my driver and do some stretching exercises. I place the club across my upper back and wrap both elbows around the shaft and do ten slow upper body turns. I then move the club to the base of my back and put one hand on the head of the driver and the other on the grip and do another ten turns.

12. I then take a few practice swings with the driver to check the path of the clubhead as it passes through the hitting area. There is usually some long grass around the practice green or first tee where I can perform these swings. While I take these swings I watch how the grass moves as the clubhead travels through it. The movement of the grass indicates my swing path.

13. I wrap up the warmup by taking a few more practice swings with the driver. I start out with slow long swings and gradually progress to swinging as hard as I can. I do not stop a swing after completing it. I finish one swing and bring the club all the way back to the top of my backswing and go through it again. This builds up a good momentum and I believe, stretches my muscles better. I keep swinging the club until I have completed about ten swings.

As I mentioned this warmup routine usually takes 20 minutes. Sometimes I do not finish the whole routine. When short of time I cut down the putting and chipping segments. If I have more time, perhaps due to the tee times being late, I hit a few more putts.

If a driving range is nearby and I feel like making the effort (I rarely do) I may hit a few shots. At the most I hit ten three quarter wedge shots just to help me loosen up. If I hit any more I get tired later in the round.

I try to make sure I have the time for this warmup session. This is why I like to play at a course that assigns tee times so I can schedule this time.

I do find it annoying when the tee is empty and my playing partners want to tee off early. Because I have to cut back on my warmup routine this disturbs me and although I usually give in, I do not like it.

Now to the first tee. All keen and ready to go. The only thought I have here is to remind myself to stay calm and relaxed. If I felt rushed before, I clear my mind. It is then time to talk with your partners and make the bets.

SECTION 15.5 — DRILLS

There are two drills I go through at least once every two weeks. They only take a few minutes each.

1.   The first drill is designed to check the ball position and alignment. I perform this drill on a tiled floor or any floor with crossing straight lines. This drill consists of going through the following sequence with each club:

1.1 I place the sole of the club on the floor with the leading edge square to one of the lines.

1.2 I carefully take my normal stance for that club.

1.3 I then visually check the following:

- The clubface is square to the line. I ensure I have not turned the clubface offline while taking my stance. I am very careful with this because my irons appear to be slightly closed when they are actually square to the line. My woods appear to be slightly open. Checking this reinforces how the correct alignment should look.

- The ball position in my stance. I follow the line the clubface is aligned to and see where it is relative to my left (forward) heel.

- The width of my stance. My stance is narrower for a wedge than for a driver. Over time I have learned the correct width for each club.

- My feet are square to the line. I do this by looking at where my toes are relative to the line which crosses my toes. This tells me how I am naturally setting up my feet. Occasionally I find I am setting up with my left (leading) foot a little open or behind the line.

- When these checks are finished, I note the appearance of the clubface, the ball position and the feel of the overall set up. By the feel of the setup I mean how far bent over I am, how far my hands are from my body and the angle of my wrists. I concentrate on these positions in order to "program" the proper appearance

139

and feel for that club into my brain. This way it becomes automatic on the course.

2. My second drill is designed to check the other factors involved in setting up to the ball correctly. It includes addressing the ball with each club in front of a full-length mirror. If you do not have a full-length mirror, this drill can be done in front of a glass door at night, for example a patio door. With the lights on you can see your reflection in the glass. This drill involves performing the following sequence with each club:

2.1 The first part of the drill involves setting up to an imaginary ball with the mirror on the right. This gives me a view where I can see if my hands are too far from my body and my feet, hips and shoulders are square. If there is room for a swing, I check my backswing is not too flat or upright.

While looking in the mirror it is difficult to make a perfect swing so make allowances. Also be careful not to hit anything, or anyone with the club. Especially be careful of small children who when they see this, certainly will be curious, if not wonder if you have some kind of mental problem. Adults who see this may also wonder the same thing.

2.2 Next I turn 180 degrees so the mirror is on my left and repeat the checks.

2.3 I turn 90 degrees and face the mirror. Here I check my left shoulder is slightly above my right shoulder, my arms are at the proper angle, my left arm is straight, my weight looks evenly balanced and my feet are the proper distance apart. I then take a slow swing and watch my left arm to ensure I am keeping it relatively straight. On the downswing I watch my knees and legs to ensure they are moving properly.

That is all for my bi-weekly drills.

SECTION 15.6 — EXERCISE ROUTINE

During the golf season, on almost every day I do not play golf, I do my exercises. My routine takes about 10 minutes and is not extensive. It is a light routine and not a workout. I use an exercise bike and a set of weights.

As I am not an expert in this area I will not discuss the exercises I go through. The golf magazines frequently have articles that include exercises recommended by experts. You need to be careful with the exercises you choose so you do not injure yourself. Develop your own program and stick to it.

SECTION 15.7 — PRACTICE ROUTINES

At least once every two weeks I have a practice session. What I practice depends on the state of my game at the time. Each of these sessions is described below.

SUBSECTION 15.7.1 — FULL SHOT PRACTICE ROUTINE

When I go to the driving range I may practice full shots with a number of clubs or work on one or two specific clubs.

Even though I do have a shag bag full of practice balls I prefer to go a driving range because I like to hit irons off the mats at the range. I find I hit more good shots off these mats and this improves my confidence.

Practising on good flat lies allows me to correctly diagnose any problems. If I hit off a bad lie and get a bad result I am not sure if the cause was my swing or the bad lie. With a good lie I cannot blame the lie, I know it was my swing.

By the way, if I do decide to practice unusual shots like downhill shots, I do so only when my swing is in solid shape. If the swing is not good I have a minimal chance of hitting difficult shots well.

When I go to the range I usually buy a large bucket with about eighty balls. I will only get a small bucket, forty or fifty balls, when I am working on a specific problem and have limited time.

I prefer not to practice when there is a strong crosswind in either direction. With a crosswind the ball can be moved and I do not get the proper feedback from the shot. If I do decide to practice in these conditions I do not watch the ball at the end of its flight.

My practice routine at the driving range is as follows:
1. I first find a stall where the mat for irons is in good condition and the rubber tee at the height I want.
2. I lay ten balls in a line from front to back on the far edge of the mat. I lay these balls out so I do not have to keep picking balls out of the bucket. I admit to being lazy, but this also helps to speed up the time between shots and I feel, helps me find a rhythm.
3. To start off I take out my 8 iron, my favorite club, and do a few stretching exercises. I also take a few practice swings.
4. Next I determine where on the mat I will be hitting the ball. I want a level lie.
5. I then hit the ten balls laid out on the mat, starting with a slow smooth swing and gradually increasing the speed to a normal full 8 iron shot. After each shot I use the clubface to move one of the balls already on

the mat to the hitting area. Many people like to pause between shots and think about the last shot. I do a quick diagnosis between shots but do not spend any length of time thinking about it. I do my analysis after I have hit the group of ten shots. After I have hit my first ten shots with the 8 iron my warmup is complete.

6.   I then decide either to hit another ten with my 8 iron or go to another club. My decision depends what I am trying to achieve in this session. If it is a general tuneup session I hit a 5 iron next, then a 3 iron, a fairway wood and finally a driver. I hit at least one group of ten shots with each club. If I am not hitting a specific club well I hit a second group of ten with it.

7.   If I am trying to correct a specific problem with one club or a number of clubs, when I get to a problem club I go back to basics. I do the following:

- I carefully review my setup. This includes hand position, posture, stance, grip and ball position. This check is similar to the checks I go through in my drills. Occasionally I find some error has crept into my game with this club.
- I take a few practice swings. I try to "feel" if there is anything wrong. By "feel" I mean sensing if the swing with this club feels different to a swing with another club. I stop my swing at points to check the position of my hands, arms and legs. Sometimes I find something is wrong here.
- I review any special swing keys I have for this club.
- If I still have not found the problem I hit a group of ten balls using my soft swing.
- I analyze the results. Often I know immediately what is wrong and can correct it. If I do not, I think of the problem and try any remedies that seem appropriate.

When I look at the results of my shots I look at the trajectory, height and velocity of the ball. I usually do not watch the ball land. I also pay attention to the feel of the shot. I know what a good shot feels like and I watch for this feel. When using an iron on driving range mats I listen to the sound at impact. When I hit a shot well I hear a squeaking noise, not a clunk.

If after this second group of ten shots I am still having problems, I begin to experiment. I may change my tempo by starting the downswing with my arms rather than my legs, or I may break my wrists early in the backswing, or I may swing harder or softer. I try anything I can think of for a few shots and watch the results. I continue until I fix the problem or run out of practice balls. I may end up with a new swing key with this specific club.

If I have not fixed the problem after the first session and the problem is with many clubs, I consult the swing remedies in the Jack Nicklaus books I mentioned in Stage 3. I then try the appropriate remedy at my next practice session.

If I have a persistent problem with only one club, I apply lead tape to the offending club and have another session.

If I have not fixed the problem after two practice sessions, I stop the sessions but continue to try to fix the problem by making adjustments while I am playing.

It is unusual for me not to fix a problem during the practice sessions. Just going back to basics and checking everything carefully fixes most problems. The remedy does not need to produce perfect shots just reasonable shots reasonably consistently. I never search for perfection. I know I will novor find it.

I have had times when I hit the ball great at the range but poorly on the course. This is very frustrating. When this happens I am patient and wait for my on course improvement to come. Eventually it does, even though it can take longer than I would like. I do not know why this happens but I suspect when I am at the range I develop a rhythm of hitting the ball well and on the course I lose the benefit of repeating the same swing with the same club in a short time.

8.   If I have solved the problem I came to work on and still have balls left or I get tired I go into a shutdown routine. I also like to quit on a positive note because it helps reinforce my confidence. So if I only have a few balls left and am hitting the ball great, I also go into my shutdown routine.

My shutdown routine consists of hitting all the remaining balls with half and three quarter wedge shots. If I do not have my wedge I use the highest club there. I hit these shots softly and concentrate on my body movements as I hit the ball. I consciously consider the weight transfer, movement of the arms, turning of the upper body, etc. This helps improve my timing and tempo.

This completes the full shot practice session.

If I have had a bad session I will make time for another practice session within the next few days. I find the quality of my shots deteriorate after the first bucket so any further practice during this session would be a waste of time. I admire the dedication and tenacity of the people who hit balls for hours, but it just does not work for me.

In my full shot practice session I do not have any regular games I play. I may try to hook or slice the ball and hit some shots high and others low, but that is as far as I go. If you find the above routine boring, you can play any number of practice games. Use your imagination and try a few. Practice must be enjoyable.

SUBSECTION 15.7.2 — SAND SHOT PRACTICE ROUTINE

I do not do a lot in this routine, I just experiment and watch the results. The steps in this routine are:

1.   In the bunker I place six balls in a row, about 4 inches (10 centimetres) apart.

2.   I then hit the group of six balls, rake the sand, retrieve the balls and hit another group. I hit a number of shots with the face of the sand wedge wide open and some with the face at varying degrees of open and closed. I hit shots where the club strikes the sand a few inches (centimetres) behind the ball and where the club strikes the sand immediately behind the ball. I will also play some shots from buried lies. I note the results of the different shots I have played.

3.   I quit when I feel comfortable with the results. I usually only practice sand play a couple of times a season. I am a good sand player and am happy with my skill level.

SUBSECTION 15.7.3 — CHIPPING PRACTICE ROUTINE

I practice chip shots over and above my warmup routine, about once every month. These are scoring shots so it is important I maintain my touch and feel for distances. The steps I follow in this routine are:

1.   I start the routine with three balls and my sand wedge. The first task is a quick check of my setup. The things I check include:

- My stance is narrow and slightly open.
- My weight is on my left side.
- The ball is positioned off my right (back) heel. With the ball back the chance of hitting the shot fat is reduced. I prefer to hit a chip thin rather than fat. A chip shot hit thin will still advance, although perhaps too far, but a shot hit fat may only go a few inches (centimetres).
- My hands are forward and my wrists bent.
- I keep my wrists firm through the stroke.

These checks ensure I am setting up to the ball properly and hitting the shots in the manner I prefer.

2.   I then hit a number of chip shots with the sand wedge and continue until I am happy with the results. This usually requires hitting four or five groups of three balls. With the sand wedge I practice chip shots of between 10 and 20 feet (3 to 6 metres), including roll.

3.   I next change to a 9 iron and hit a number of chip shots in the 20 to 40 foot (7 to 12 metre) range.

4.   I then take my 8 iron and practice chip shots in the 40 to 60 foot (13 to 18 metre) range.

5.   When I am happy with the results, I quit. I may finish by going back to the sand wedge and hitting very short chip shots of 10 feet (3 metres) or less. Hitting these short shots requires a slow, smooth swing which helps develop my touch and feel, and ensures I do not quit during the stroke.

When practicing chip shots I aim at a specific hole in the putting green but I do not line the shot up as I would on the course. I just drop the balls on the fringe and line up by sight as I address the ball.

This completes the chipping routine. My chipping practice sessions usually take less than half an hour.

SUBSECTION 15.7.4 — PUTTING PRACTICE ROUTINE

I go through my putting practice routine whenever I feel like it. I try to have at least one session per month. Putting is a vital part of the game and it is important I am putting well.

My putting practice routine is different from my other routines. I go through a setup check only if I am having problems. The checks I perform in my pre-round routine are usually sufficient to ensure my setup is correct.

The steps within this routine are:

1.   I take the putter I am currently using and a group of three balls. I hit a few warmup putts to get the feel of my putting stroke and the speed of the green. This usually consists of three or four groups of balls. I do not line up these putts, I just hit them to one of the holes on the green.

2.   I play a game which consists of hitting three balls to each of nine holes on the green. I choose the holes as I go along and vary the distances from 8 to 30 feet (3 to 9 metres). I do not spend any time lining up the putts, I just aim as I address the ball. I keep track of my score using a "par" of two putts per ball per hole, and relate my score to this base. As I go along I remember how many over or under I am.

3.   I do a number of rounds of these nine holes, with three balls per hole, until I finish with a score of three under or better. I do not quit until I make this score. Or it rains.

Usually this session takes just over half an hour. I frequently combine it with a chipping session. Together they take about an hour.

SUBSECTION 15.7.5 — END OF PRACTICE ROUTINES

Those are the routines I go through during my practice sessions. I try to have at least one practice session every two weeks during the season. If I have a specific problem I may try to correct it with an extra session as needed. At least once a month I have a chipping and putting session. As I have said these are the real scoring shots and must be treated as such.

Occasionally if I have some spare time I may decide to have an extra practice session and work on some part of my game. I enjoy playing golf and practicing.

Remember, the results of your practice sessions take time to show up in your game. This is just the way things are. Be patient.

SECTION 15.8 — WINTER ROUTINE

As I have mentioned I played most of my golf in Canada. In the winter there is snow on the ground and it can be incredibly cold. The routine I have developed to keep my game in some form of reasonable shape over the winter consists of:

1.   Swinging a weighted club at least three times a week. I swing the club until I feel a little tired. The more often I do this the longer it takes to get tired. Start easy with only a few swings.

2.   Doing my exercises three times a week.

3.   Putting on my living room carpet at least once a week.

4.   Chipping plastic practice balls into a chipping basket once or twice a week. I enjoy doing this while watching television. I hit off an old carpet remnant so as not to damage the regular carpet.

5.   Playing a round of golf at PAR-T™ every Thursday. This is indoor golf where balls are hit off mats into a screen. The screen has pictures of the holes being played and after each shot a computer calculates how far the shot went. The computer then tells you how far it is to the hole and you keep hitting shots until you get on the green. You then putt the ball to a hole in the floor.

This is not regular golf, but it is certainly better than sitting around at home. Once I became familiar with the machine, I have been was able to shoot some scores in the 60's for 18 holes. It is fun.

CHAPTER 16
COURSE MANAGEMENT

Where do the shots go? You play well, make a few putts, hit a few good shots, a few mediocre shots, and no bad shots that get you into any real trouble. When you add them up at the end of the round — still too many.

If this sounds familiar, you need to look at the decisions you are making while you are playing. How are you managing your way around the course?

Course management is the managing of your individual game with your strengths and weaknesses around the golf course you are playing. Or more specifically, the one hole you are playing. This means playing the course in the best possible manner and keeping the lost shots to a minimum. In short, thinking your way around the course.

A vast number of issues must be considered with course management. The best way to explain what I have learned is to discuss the issues I consider when playing my home course. By this detailed explanation, I hope to explain by example and communicate the principles of course management as I understand them. When reading this chapter try to think of similar situations at your home course and how you can apply the same principles.

Although only a cursory description of the features of each hole is provided these are the factors and terrain conditions you should watch for. The fact you will probably never see those holes is not important, what is important is you learn to identify the playability factors.

I must point out that these principles are based on the strengths of my game as I perceive them to be. They assume I am playing at a five handicap level and in midseason form. For higher handicappers this level of analysis may not be appropriate.

When discussing each situation I do not mention all the possible weather conditions, lie factors and other such components which could affect every shot. To do so would stretch an already detailed discussion beyond the point of understanding.

Before the hole-by-hole analysis I need to explain the general rules I follow. I keep these in the back of my mind and adhere to them most of the time. The circumstances of the exact situation may cause me to plan a shot outside these rules, but they are the basic fundamentals of my course management.

Some of the principles have been mentioned in the earlier chapters. These I repeat for clarity. My fundamental course management rules are:

147

1. Keep the ball in play.
2. Play to make bogey at worst.
3. Avoid out of bounds, water hazards and dense bush at all costs.
4. Place all shots in the best POSSIBLE position for the next shot.
5. From within 150 yards (135 metres) from the middle of the green, get aggressive. I usually try to get as close to the pin as possible.
6. From 150 to 180 yards (135 to 165 metres) try to get the ball close to the pin, or depending on the situation, shoot for the middle of the green. Normally I just shoot for the center of the green. If it is a large green I aim for the portion where the pin is.
7. Outside 180 yards (165 metres) try to get the ball on or near the green. This involves aiming at the safest area, the location with the largest margin for error that avoids hazards and provides the best possible attack to the current pin position.
8. Allow for the movement of the ball after it lands.

General principles based on the type of hole, par 3's, 4's and 5's, are discussed in the HOW TO PLAY A STRANGE COURSE section later in this chapter.

As mentioned earlier, the best way I feel to communicate the course management principles as I understand them is to explain how I handle specific situations at my home course. I describe the course playing from the Blue (back) tees. The total distance is 6408 yards (5859 metres) and par is 71.

HOLE BY HOLE ANALYSIS

HOLE 1. PAR 4, 430 YARDS (393 METRES), HANDICAP 3

1.1 THE HOLE. The first hole is a slight dogleg left. The tee is elevated and the hole usually plays downwind. The fairway gently slopes left to right and there are trees down the right side and some on the left.

1.2 THE TEE SHOT. The first option, which is the ideal shot, is to hit a draw around the dogleg landing on the left side of the fairway. Since this is the first tee, because I am not fully warmed up, I do not try a fancy shot. I simply aim down the left centre and hit my normal fade to the right.

1.3 THE APPROACH. After a reasonable drive I am usually 185 to 200 yards (167 to 180 meters) from the center of the green. The ball is probably in the contour fairway with a flat lie. From this distance I try to get the ball to the safest area.

To determine the safe area look at the terrain surrounding the green. The green has two bunkers on the left and one on the right.

The left bunkers are shallow and the right bunker is deep and has a large lip. The right bunker should be avoided, especially when the pin is on the right.

The green slopes sharply from back to front. Behind the green is a severe downslope with dense bush beyond. From behind, even if the ball stops before the bushes, a tricky high wedge shot is required. With the slope of the green being away from the shot, it is difficult to get close to the hole.

The terrain in front of the green slopes to the right. A shot just short of the green to the left will usually bounce to the right, sometimes onto the green. A shot short and to the right will usually run into the bunker. The safe area is the left front of the green.

If I am 185 yards (169 metres) away I hit a soft 3 iron. This shot, if hit well, will land on the very front of the green or just in front. If the ball stops short of the green I have an uphill chip shot, which is not too difficult. If on the green, I usually have an uphill putt.

If I am 200 yards (184 metres) out I hit a 5 wood, but softly. I am careful because if I catch the 5 wood well the ball may go over the back.

If I am 190 to 195 yards (173 to 178 metres) out I have a problem. I do not hit my 3 iron this far and I hit the 5 wood farther. I may decide to cut a soft 5 wood or hit the 3 iron hard. My choice depends on whether the ball is sitting up or down in the grass. If I have a good lie with the ball sitting up, I hit the 3 iron. If the ball is sitting down I use the 5 wood.

Usually I would prefer not to hit a cut 5 wood shot on the first hole. When I am not warmed up, fancy shots like this have a lower probability of success. However in this case, if the shot does not turn out well, the ball will probably end up in front of the green and I will have an easy flip wedge shot. This worst case result makes the shot an option.

1.4 ON THE GREEN. Due to the sharp back to front slope there is a lot of break on this green. If I am below the hole and within 20 feet (6 metres) I try to make the putt but am careful not to go too far past the hole. I do not want a tricky downhill slider for a comeback putt.

For downhill and sidehill putts, if I am more than 10 feet (3 metres) away I still try to make the putt but my main concern is to get the ball close to the hole. These are tricky putts and very difficult to make.

This hole plays a little longer than the distance on the card, mainly because I hit my tee shot to the right and this is the long way to play the hole. I should make 4 or 5, a bogey is not a bad score.

HOLE 2. PAR 5, 505 YARDS (462 METRES), HANDICAP 1

2.1 THE HOLE. The second hole is a slight dogleg left. For the first 250 yards (230 metres) the fairway is generally flat and for the next 240 yards (220 metres) it rises at a steep incline of 30 to 40 degrees. The slope levels out just in front of the green. In the tee shot landing area on the left is a fairway bunker and on the right a group of trees.

2.2 THE TEE SHOT. This hole is out of my range in two shots. On the tee I just try to pick the best spot to give me an easy second shot. To have an easy second shot I have to know where I want to hit my third shot from. The position I want to hit my third shot from usually depends on the pin position. However, on this hole, because of the subsequent hazards (discussed later) these hazards become the overriding consideration.

From the tee I am trying to place my ball on the right side of the fairway. This avoids the fairway bunker and gives me the best approach to the spot I want for my third shot. I do however, not want to go too far right for two reasons. First the fairway is hard on this side and the ball may roll into the trees. Second the ground near the trees is usually in bad shape and there is a good chance of getting a bad lie. By bad lie I mean the ball sitting down on bare ground and tufts of grass behind and/or in front of the ball.

It is my opinion this area should be marked as ground under repair when in this condition. The grass does not grow well because of trees blocking the sunlight and the maintenance staff driving their vehicles over the area. I do not mean to criticize the greens staff, I only bring up this point to give you an idea of what to look for.

2.3 THE SECOND SHOT. The ball is usually sitting on a level part of the fairway. My main consideration is to end up less than 120 yards (110 metres) from the middle of the green and on the left side. The incline of the fairway on the left is not as severe. I want to give myself as easy a shot as possible.

Playing to the left also takes the right fairway bunkers out of play. A fairway bunker shot of between 50 and 90 yards (45 and 80 metres) is a hard shot for me, especially to a green elevated far above the level of the bunker.

To get to my target area I can hit either a normal 4 wood or a soft 3 wood. In most cases when I have a choice I choose the longer club and hit it softly. Here is an exception. There are two reasons for the exception. First, I do not hit my 3 wood off the fairway unless I have a perfect lie or if I need extra distance. Second, I simply prefer to hit my 4 wood because I find it an easier club to hit.

If there is no real benefit to be gained always choose the easier club to hit over the harder club. Or another way of looking at this is choose a strength of your game over a weakness.

2.4 THE APPROACH. The upwards slope of the fairway levels out just in front of the green. Beside the green on the left is a small hill and further left, out of bounds. To the right is a cart path, bush and a sharp downslope. The green itself is very narrow but long. The green slopes generally from left to right. The right front portion has a knoll that can deflect the ball off the green. Overall a small target area with severe penalties if missed.

The ball is probably between 70 and 90 yards (60 to 80 metres) from the middle of the green. The pin position now becomes a major concern. I check how far back the pin is and adjust my distance and target area accordingly.

Usually I use my pitching wedge and hit what I feel to be the correct distance. Because I have an uphill stance, and the green is above me, I hit the shot harder than normal for a shot of the same distance. I also consider how much the ball will roll after it lands. This depends on the anticipated trajectory of the shot and how well the greens are holding.

This green has some difficult spots to putt to. I have seen pin placements where a putt cannot be made unless the approach is from the correct side.

This hole plays much longer than the distance on the card due mainly to the severe upward incline of the fairway. I expect to make 4 or 5 on this hole.

HOLE 3. PAR 3, 144 YARDS (131 METRES), HANDICAP 17

3.1 THE HOLE. The third is a short downhill par 3. Left of the green is a hill sloping down towards and projecting partly out in front of the green. If the pin is behind the hill an optical illusion is created making the pin appear closer than it is.

Out of bounds is on both sides and at the back. On the left the out of bounds does not normally come into play, but at the back and to the right it can be a factor, especially on a windy day.

3.2 THE TEE SHOT. The main problem here is club selection. This depends on the pin position, tee position, weather, etc. I have hit everything from a wedge to a 5 iron. A ball landing on the right third of this green will usually roll off. A ball landing anywhere else on this green will usually stop quickly. If there is any roll the ball will go to the right.

Playing this hole on a windy day is tricky. When standing on the tee you are shielded from the wind by surrounding trees. The green is also shielded by bushes so the direction the flag is pointing may not be correct. To determine the wind direction I look at the top of high trees to see which way they are being blown. I then know the wind direction up in the air where the ball will be.

3.3 ON The GREEN. Putts on the front part of this green tend to break more than at the back. I do not know why, I just remember to allow for more break on the front.

This hole plays shorter than the distance on the card, mainly because the green is below the level of the tee. I expect to make 3 on this hole, maybe 2.

HOLE 4. PAR 4, 293 YARDS (268 METRES), HANDICAP 15

4.1 THE HOLE. The fourth is a straight downhill par 4. The tee is elevated 50 feet (15 metres) above the fairway. On the left is an out of bounds fence which runs the complete length of the hole. This fence is definitely in play, I have put many a tee shot over this fence. Near the green it is only a few yards (metres) from the left edge. Right of the fairway is a large hill sloping towards the fairway.

The green has a bunker at the right front and another two in front on the left. On both the left and right of the fairway, a little back from the bunkers are small groups of trees. The fairway has a distinct slope from right to left.

4.2 THE TEE SHOT. This hole is a very short par 4 and the elevated tee makes it play shorter. On the tee a person has to make the choice of going for the green or laying up. I discussed the way I play this tee shot earlier in the Stage 4 and Stage 5 chapters. Essentially I stopped trying to go for the green because I was scoring too high when I did so.

The way I now play this hole is to lay up with a 4 wood. This will leave the ball short of the trees on either side. The question is how far to the right I should hit the shot.

If the pin is on the left I want my ball to be on the right side of the fairway. In this case I hit the shot into the hill and let it roll down to the right side. There is a very large margin for error here as the hill is quite high and steep, so if I push or pull the shot even by a fair amount the ball will still end up in the target area.

I like this type of shot. No pressure and a wide margin for error. A shot like this has a high probability of success. Part of course management is identifying the potential for increasing the margin of error and making the game easier to play. Analysis of a hole, keeping risks to a minimum and placing yourself in a position to hit shots in which you are confident you can play well, is the essence of effective course management.

Occasionally I get sloppy with this tee shot. I have it figured out so well and am so confident it is an easy shot, I sometimes forget to prepare properly. This is a mental error I need to watch out for.

If the pin is on the right I want my ball to be on the left side of the fairway. I then move my target area to the left. The terrain slopes right to left and the ball will kick left when it lands. So I aim at the right edge of the fairway and let the terrain take the ball to the left side. Another easy shot with a large margin for error.

If the pin is on the right, tucked close to the front bunker I want my approach shot to come from the far left side of the fairway. This is because the terrain slopes from the bunker down and well onto the green and this part of the green tends to be hard. From the left I can cut the ball into the slope and stop it quicker. This gives me a higher probability of getting the ball close to the hole.

When the pin is on the front left the best approach angle is the far right. This gives me more green to work with (land on) and a wider target area. If the greens are firm I can land the shot well short of the pin and let it roll up.

4.3 THE APPROACH. The ball is usually about 75 yards (67 metres) from the middle of the green. The lie is very good because hardly anyone hits to this area, most try to get the ball as close to the green as possible. Therefore the area in front of the bunkers gets a lot of wear and tear.

For my approach the ball is most likely slightly above my feet. I do not hit the ball as far from an abnormal stance such as this, so I hit the shot a little harder. Also from this lie the shot will tend to be pulled (or go left) slightly offline. On a long shot the ball will hook or draw. I compensate by aiming a little right of my target.

With my laying up off the tee, the ball is in approximately the same position every time. This has the result of my knowing, over playing the hole a number of times, how hard to hit my partial wedge shot to the pin. Even though the pin was in different positions I became familiar with how hard to hit the ball to a specific area from this spot. This has increased the accuracy of my approach shots resulting in an increase in the number of birdies.

There is a trouble shot I sometimes need on this hole. I have, on occasion, hit the ball too far left off the tee. If I am lucky enough to have the ball bounce off the fence, it usually stops close to the fence. Since I am right handed, I cannot take a full swing.

I first check if there is room to bring the club back far enough to generate the power required to get the ball to the green. If there is, I hit the ball this way, probably with a restricted backswing.

If not, I hit a left handed shot. To hit this shot I take a left handed stance and normal left handed grip. Some people may prefer to hit this shot crosshanded. I then take the club and turn it so the toe of the club is on the ground and the heel is up in the air. Or, to explain how to get the club in the correct position another way, take the club and place it on the ground normally. Using a spot on the grip as a reference point, rotate the grip 180 degrees.

This puts the club in a position where you can hit the ball. With the clubface set as above the shot will be hit in the direction the clubface is pointing, to the right about 45 degrees. To hit the shot high or more on the direction of your alignment, rotate the club further to the left. The only clubs I hit left handed are short irons or a 5 wood. These all have fairly large faces and enough loft to get the ball up.

This shot, once mastered can be hit with some accuracy. I frequently use it to advance the ball back into a playable position. However, on this hole I can hit the green with some regularity. I hit one shot of about 60 yards (55 metres) to 3 feet (1 metre) from the hole using this technique. It was a good shot, but a fluke. I did however expect to get the ball on the green.

This hole plays considerably shorter than the distance on the card, primarily due to the extreme drop in elevation. I consider this a hole that should be birdied. A par is acceptable, a bogey terrible, double bogey is heave the ball away time.

HOLE 5. PAR 4, 380 YARDS (347 METRES), HANDICAP 11

5.1 THE HOLE. The fifth hole is a slight dogleg left. There are two fairway bunkers in the landing area for the tee shot, one on each side. Trees on the left side are sparse, although a group of trees near the green can block an approach shot from the left. The green slopes from front to back away from play.

5.2 THE TEE SHOT. Off this tee I have a problem because the surrounding trees create a shute aligned to the right of the fairway. For some reason I subconsciously pick up the line of the shute and change my swing to hit the ball along the line. I do not know why this happens, I just know it does. Even if I carefully aim to the left, during the swing my subconscious will take over and I try to hit the ball to the right.

The only way I have found to stop this tendency is to make sure I do not look down the fairway once I have chosen my line and addressed the ball. Not even a quick glance. I trust I am lined up correctly and go from there. This is the worst hole on the course for this misalignment and it is especially noticeable when the tee is as far back as it can go.

5.3 THE APPROACH. I have been in the right fairway bunker many times. This is a kidney shaped bunker where the front is 165 yards (151 metres) from the middle of the green.

On the left, the lip is only a few inches (centimetres) but on the right the lip is about two feet (half a metre). A ball in the left side of the bunker can, unless it is very near the lip, be played to the green. A ball in the right side usually cannot, or at least I cannot hit the iron required to clear the lip, far enough to get to the green.

When the ball is in the left side I aim for the middle of the green. I do not get fancy with these shots. From approximately 170 yards (155 metres) out of a fairway bunker, I am happy to get the ball on or near the green.

If I am in the bunker on the right side, I take the club I know will get the ball high enough to clear the lip. This is usually a 7 or 8 iron and I hit it as far as I can, without swinging too hard. I try to put this shot in the best position for my forthcoming wedge shot. No matter what I choose to do, getting the ball out of the bunker is the first priority

My general rule for fairway bunker shots is to take one more club than normal and play the ball back an extra 2 inches (5 centimetres) in my stance. With the ball back I increase the chance of catching the ball before the sand and if I do mishit the shot I will probably hit it thin rather than fat.

A shot hit fat out of a bunker does not go very far. A shot hit thin, provided it still clears the lip, will go a fair distance and may even run onto the green. This is how I increase the probability of a better result even if I hit a mediocre shot.

With the ball back further than normal, I hit the ball to the right. To adjust I aim left. The amount I aim left depends on the club I am using, but with a 7 or 8 iron I aim about 30 feet (10 metres) left of the target.

Also with fairway bunker shots I take a very slow backswing and minimise the weight transfer back and forth during the swing. This reduces the chance of my feet sinking or moving in the sand. With stable footing I have a higher probability of returning the clubface to the ball.

As this green slopes away from play, approach shots tend to not stop quickly. I subtract 5 yards (meters) from the playing distance when planning a normal approach shot to allow for this extra roll.

5.4 ON THE GREEN. The green tends to be a little quicker than the others on the course. The back left is quicker because it gets very little sunlight and therefore the grass is thin. The right front is quicker because the path to the next tee is on this side, so it is a heavy traffic area.

I expect to make a par 4 on this hole.

HOLE 6. PAR 4, 386 YARDS (353 METRES), HANDICAP 7

6.1 THE HOLE. This hole appears to be straight away but actually plays as a slight dogleg right. The green is slightly elevated with a bunker at the right front and another on the left. To the right and behind the green is dense bush.

6.2 THE TEE SHOT. For the big hitters this is a fairly easy driving hole. They can hit the ball almost straight away and have a short iron in.

For me it is a different story. If the tee is up front I can hit down the middle and have maybe a 7 or an 8 iron in, at best. Otherwise, I have to be careful with the placement of my tee shot in order to give me an easy approach.

The best place to approach this green is the left center of the fairway because it takes the front right bunker out of play. From the left, a shot hit short, due to a mishit for example, will possibly run onto the green, whereas from the right a shot landing short will end up in the bunker.

6.3 THE APPROACH. My approach shot ranges between 150 to 180 yards (135 to 165 metres). I just try to get the ball on the middle of the green. I am happy if the ball lands anywhere on this green because the bunkers and dense bush surrounding the green can cause problems.

6.4 ON THE GREEN. This green slopes right to left. The right side is faster and has more break than the left side. I am not sure why this is so, but I suspect it has something to do with the water settling patterns. Many times the left side of this green seems to be wet while the right side is dry.

For me this hole plays slightly longer than the distance on the card. I will accept a bogey on this hole occasionally.

HOLE 7. PAR 3, 235 YARDS (215 METRES), HANDICAP 9

7.1 THE HOLE. The seventh is a very long uphill par 3. Behind the green is dense bush and to the right is a mound and a clump of bushes.

7.2 THE TEE SHOT. My strategy for this shot was discussed in Stage 5. Due to the narrowness of the landing area I use my 3 wood off the tee rather than my driver, even though I know I cannot always get to the green with this club. I play safe off the tee in order to guard against double bogey.

This is a hard hole to par, let alone birdie. I manage par sometimes, birdie rarely, but the frequency of double bogeys have been reduced.

7.3 AROUND THE GREEN. If I happen to miss my the landing area and end up in the bunker in front of this green I have a long bunker shot of up to 40 yards (35 metres) to the pin. This is a hard shot. I do not always recover well from this position.

I play the ball back off my right heel and try to hit the ball before the club strikes the sand. I use my normal partial wedge stroke with my sand wedge and hit the ball about fifty percent harder than I would if the ball was on grass. Even with this technique I am not very accurate.

I try to get the ball near the pin but guard against going over the green at all costs. If the ball goes in the dense bush I will probably make double bogey or worse. Getting the ball on the green allows me a chance of making a putt for par or bogey at worst.

For the player who can hit the ball in the air far enough to carry the front bunker, this hole is somewhat easier to play. However, it is a hard hole for every level of player. I expect to make 3 or 4. If I make a bogey I am not unhappy.

The front bunker has recently been filled in.

I have made a hole-in-one on this hole. A 3 wood hit hard and well.

HOLE 8. PAR 5, 515 YARDS (471 METERS), HANDICAP 5

8.1 THE HOLE. The eighth is a straight away par 5. An out of bounds fence runs the complete length of the hole on the left. On the right, starting from about 250 yards (225 metres) from the tee, is dense bush all the way to the green. The fairway generally slopes right to left with a pronounced slope on the left edge towards the out of bounds fence. There is also water on the right and short of the green

8.2 THE TEE SHOT. This hole is well out of my range in two shots. My main concern off the tee is not to go left, near the fence. Consequently I hit a normal drive to the right side of the fairway.

If the tee is up front, the wind is behind, and the ground is hard I have to be careful my drive does not reach the bush on the right.

8.3 THE SECOND SHOT. The landing area for the second shot is very narrow. Because I am on the right side of the fairway and aiming to the left, it is even narrower. I must at all costs avoid the out of bounds fence and the water.

The ball is usually slightly above my feet and in contour length grass. The lie with the ball above the feet can be dangerous because of an increased chance of hitting a hook over the fence. However because the ball is in longer grass the amount of sidespin is reduced. To be on the safe side I open the face of the club a little for this shot.

A trouble shot I sometimes have on this hole is when I hit my tee shot too far right onto the adjoining fairway. In this case I have to hit a blind second shot back over the bushes. This is a relatively easy shot, it just takes experience to know which line to take.

The natural tendency is to try to carry too many of the bushes by aiming too far right. I take a 5 wood, open the face to ensure I clear the bushes and aim about 10 yards (metres) to the left of where I think the line for the shot should be. This is the conservative way and will leave me a longer approach shot but it is better to be a few yards (metres) further from the green than to catch a part of a bush and end up stymied.

Before I hit the shot I ask my playing partners standing on the eighth fairway to watch where the ball goes. If I hit a bad shot and catch the bushes, at least someone has seen where the ball went. This reduces the probability of losing shots due to a lost ball.

8.4 THE APPROACH. My approach shot is usually between 120 and 90 yards (110 and 80 metres). From this distance I try to get the ball as close to the pin as possible. The lie is almost always uphill, downhill or sidehill, so a proper adjustment must be made.

This hole plays slightly longer than the distance on the card mainly due to the uneven fairway. It is unusual to get a level lie for either the second or the approach shot. I expect to make 4 or 5.

HOLE 9. PAR 4, 361 YARDS (335 METRES), HANDICAP 13

9.1 THE HOLE. This is an uphill dogleg left with three fairway bunkers in the tee shot landing area, one on the left and two on the right. The green is elevated and has two front bunkers, one on each side. Behind the green is an incline rising 40 feet (12 metres). There are trees lining both sides of the hole all the way to the green.

9.2 THE TEE SHOT. The fairway bunkers are very much in play off the tee. Nothing unusual here, I aim slightly right of the left bunker and let my shot fade back to the fairway.

9.3 THE APPROACH. The green is elevated by about 6 feet (2 metres) so I use one more club than normal. The green is sloped towards the player and usually holds an approach shot very well. All I have to do is be sure I hit the ball far enough to carry the bunkers.

Caution is required when there is a left to right wind. Due to the tree line and the hill behind the green, a wind from this direction will funnel at the very front of the green and can dramatically affect the ball. I have had many shots blown into the right front bunker by such a wind. In this case I hit a low punch shot just trying to get the ball on the middle of the green.

This hole plays about the same as the distance on the card. I expect to make 3, 4 or 5. I accept an occasional bogey. Although it is not a hard hole it can be tricky, especially with a crosswind.

HOLE 10. PAR 4, 378 YARDS (346 METRES), HANDICAP 10

10.1 THE HOLE. The tenth is straight away and slightly downhill. A fairway bunker on the left definitely comes into play. There is water further down the fairway but it is out of my range. The green has two bunkers on the left and one on the right. Immediately behind the green is very dense bush. The green is very narrow.

10.2 THE TEE SHOT. The main concern here is to hit to the right in order to avoid the fairway bunker. The green is also angled to accept a shot from the right.

10.3 THE APPROACH. My approach shot is frequently around 120 to 130 yards (110 to 119 metres). If I am on the right I will have a flat level lie. From this distance I try to get the ball close to the hole.

If the pin is tucked close to one of the bunkers I aim a little further away on the non-bunker side of the pin. This gives me more room for error. If the pin is at the rear my main concern is not to go over the back. The bush behind the green is so thick it is almost impossible to get the ball on the green. If the pin is up front I am careful not to land the ball in front of the green. This is a low spot on the course and therefore a water settling area. It is frequently wet and the ball will usually stop dead and not bounce onto the green.

10.4 ON THE GREEN. The green has a slight slope from back to front but this slope is not as severe as it appears. An optical illusion is created because the surrounding terrain slopes in the other direction.

This hole plays a little shorter than the distance on the card because it is slightly downhill. I expect to make a 3 or a 4.

HOLE 11. PAR 4, 381 YARDS (348 METRES), HANDICAP 8

11.1 THE HOLE. The eleventh is a straight away par 4. On the left is an out of bounds fence from tee to green. This fence is in play for both the tee shot and the approach. On both sides of the fairway trees and bushes run the complete length of the hole.

11.2 THE TEE SHOT. The landing area for the drive is much smaller than it appears from the tee. An optical illusion is created because the trees and bushes on both sides narrow at the beginning of the landing area. I do not hit my driver at full force on this hole, I ease off a bit and hit it softly. I give up distance for accuracy.

11.3 THE APPROACH. My usual approach distance is from 160 to 180 yards (145 to 165 metres). I am trying to get the ball to the middle of the green.

My worry here is not to miss the green to the right or the left. To the left, close to the green is the out of bounds fence. To the right is a downslope that can deflect a ball into bushes.

In a crosswind I have to be especially careful. When standing on the fairway the strength of a crosswind at the green can be hard to judge. Both the fairway and the green are shielded. With a strong crosswind I hit a soft 3 or 4 iron in order to keep the ball below the tops of the trees and take advantage of the shielding effect. This soft shot will probably land in front of the green and roll on.

This shot also increases the probability of not going out of bounds or being deflected into the bush. If this short shot is off line, the longer grass beside the green may stop the ball before it gets to the trouble. If the shot is on line, it will land in the fairway length grass and roll onto the green. This is one way longer grass can be used to the players advantage.

A trouble shot I frequently have is where I have hit my tee shot too far right and I need to bring the ball back through the trees. Most of the trees on this hole are evergreens with branches that start about a yard (metre) above the ground. A ball will not go through the branches because of the thickness of the needles.

Shooting over the trees is sometimes a possibility but because they are very tall I have to be quite a distance from them to clear the treetops. I am not normally this far offline. My only alternative is to hit around or under the branches.

In this situation the shot I play is a cut 3 iron. I use the 3 iron to keep the ball below the branches and cut the shot so the ball will slice around the trees and back towards the green. I choose to slice the ball rather than hook because I am more confident I can execute and control the slice.

I rarely try to reach the green with this shot because I would have to hit the club almost full strength. As I will be aiming to the left, at the out of bounds fence, I do not want to take the risk the ball will not slice as much as I expect and go over the fence. I hit the ball hard enough to slice but not so hard that it will reach the fence. The ball should end up within wedge distance in front of the green.

For some reason I like this hole and usually play it reasonably well. I have a lot of respect for the difficulty and always concentrate extra hard on every shot. I expect to make a 3 or 4. An occasional 5 does not bother me.

HOLE 12. PAR 3, 216 YARDS (196 METRES), HANDICAP 12

12.1 THE HOLE. The twelfth is a difficult, slightly uphill par 3. There are bunkers on each side of the green and an out of bounds fence on both sides and at the back. The fence on the left is only a few yards (metres) from the edge of the green and on the right it is about 20 yards (metres) from the edge.

12.2 THE TEE SHOT. On a shot of this distance I am trying to get the ball on or near the green. My primary concern is the out of bounds fence, the pin position does not matter.

My bail out area is to the right of the green because there is a little more room for error on this side. Therefore, I aim at the right side of the green, as opposed to the center.

As on the previous hole, this hole can be very difficult when it is windy. Both run in the same direction so I carefully note the affect of a head or tailwind on my shots and my playing partners' shots on the 11th. I use this knowledge to estimate the effect of the wind on the 12th.

12.3 AROUND THE GREEN. If I miss this green, which I do more often than not, I am usually to the right with a flip wedge shot over a bunker. My primary concern is not to dump the shot in the bunker, getting close to the pin is secondary. This way I ensure the worst I make is bogey, possibly par, but never double bogey.

This hole plays about the same distance as stated on the card. It is a very difficult hole for even the best players. If I make 2 I am pleased, 3 I am happy, and with 4 I am not unhappy.

HOLE 13. PAR 5, 511 YARDS (467 METRES), HANDICAP 14

13.1 THE HOLE. The 13th is a straight away par 5. Trees and bushes line both sides of the fairway, with some gaps. There are two fairway bunkers both on the left, one in the landing area for the tee shot and the other in the area for the second shot. The terrain of the fairway is rolling and slopes to the left. The tee shot landing area is wide but the fairway narrows dramatically as it nears the green.

13.2 THE TEE SHOT. My first thought is to decide whether to go for the green in two. This is the one par 5 on the course I have a chance of reaching. If I am playing well, there is a moderate tailwind and the fairway is firm I think about it.

If I do go for the green in two my tee shot must be on the left side of the fairway. To reach this green my second shot will land about 50 yards (45 metres) in front of the green and run the remaining distance. The terrain in this area slopes sharply to the left. If I approach from the right side the ball will be deflected by the terrain to the left of the green. From the left the ball will run onto the green if it comes in at the correct angle.

If I am not going for the green in two, my main consideration becomes pin placement. I look at the pin position and work backwards. If the pin is on the right I want to hit my approach from the left of the fairway. If I want my approach to be from the left I want to hit my second shot from the right. Therefore my drive must be on the right side of the fairway. If the pin is on the left the positions are reversed. This gives me the largest target areas and therefore the largest margin for error. With the approach shot I have more green to work with.

A golfing buddy occasionally liked to make bets for longest drive on this hole. As I hit my tee shots low without much carry and he hit his high, I would normally accept this bet only when the wind was blowing into us and the fairways were firm. This was my only chance of beating him. I still lost more times than I won, but it was fun.

I would accept this bet on this hole because it has the widest landing area on the course and my score would probably not be affected. My score is more important than winning a single bet.

When hitting a long drive I ignored the pin position and tried to avoid landing into an upslope in the fairway. This meant I had to hit the ball to the right side where it would get the most roll.

13.3 THE SECOND SHOT. For my second shot I try to place the ball in the position I decided off the tee. If I am aiming to the right, my main concern is to avoid the trees and if I am aiming to the left, to avoid the fairway bunker.

As I mentioned earlier the fairway narrows dramatically as it approaches the green. To reduce the chance of ending up in the trees when aiming to the right, I hit a soft 4 or 5 wood rather than a 3 wood. With the shorter distance club if I do hit it slightly offline the ball may not go far enough to get to the trees. The shorter shot also allows me to use the longer contour fairway grass to help stop an errant shot.

If I am aiming to the left I lay up behind the fairway bunker. I know from measuring the course how far I am from the bunker. I estimate the amount of roll the ball will take based on the amount of roll of my previous fairway shots. The back of this bunker is 98 yards (89 metres) from the middle of the green and even if I lay up some distance back I still have a short approach shot. The area short of this bunker is also level and usually in good shape.

If my second shot must be hit from the fairway bunker in the tee shot landing area, I change from trying to place the ball in the best position to advancing the ball and getting it to the best possible position.

This is not a difficult shot, the sand is firm and the lip is low. I use a 5 wood, play the ball back in my stance, open the face slightly and allow for a push. Even if I do not hit the shot perfectly the ball usually goes far enough to be able to get to the green with my next shot. Using a 5 wood for this shot also increases the margin for error. If I hit the shot a bit fat the wood will bounce off the sand and catch enough of the ball to advance it. I just have to ensure the ball clears the lip of the bunker, which is very low, and I do not hit the shot too far right.

13.4 THE APPROACH. This green has two bunkers both at the front, one on each side. These bunkers only come into play when trying to hit the green in two or if the pin is at the front.

This hole plays shorter than the distance on the card because it is slightly downhill and usually downwind. This is not a difficult hole. I expect to make 4 or 5. If I make 6 I am angry.

HOLE 14. PAR 4, 402 YARDS (368 METRES), HANDICAP 4

14.1 THE HOLE. The fourteenth is a straightaway uphill par 4. Trees and bushes line the left side of the fairway and sporadic trees line the right. There is a fairway bunker on the left and to the far right is a small practice fairway.

14.2 THE TEE SHOT. This is a hard hole for me. For some reason, it always plays long. With the tee back and into a headwind on a cool wet day I may be struggling to get to the green in two. This is one of the few holes I need to hit a long tee shot. My approach will be a long one so I do not consider the pin position.

I aim to the right side of the fairway in order to avoid the fairway bunker and because there is extra room on this side. With the sporadic trees on the right, I hope my shot does not end up close to any of them. If so I accept it.

14.3 THE APPROACH. The green has two tiers and is very long and narrow. There are bunkers on each side and lots of room over the back. The green retains water and holds a long approach shot very well. The terrain in front of the green is flat, so a shot hit short usually runs onto the green.

14.4 ON THE GREEN. The green was built a few years ago when a freeway was constructed through the course. This green, and the 15th green have a different base and the playing characteristics (speed and break) are different when compared to the other greens.

As I mentioned, this hole plays much longer than the distance on the card and I really do not know why. It is a hard hole for me. I accept a 4 or a bogey 5 and walk away.

HOLE 15. PAR 4, 337 YARDS (308 METRES), HANDICAP 16

15.1 THE HOLE. The fifteenth plays as a dogleg because three large evergreen trees project out onto the right side of the fairway. They are 100 yards (90 metres) from the middle of the green and about 40 feet (12 metres) high. Immediately left of the fairway, a small hill slopes gently towards the short cut.

The green is angled to the right at about 45 degrees (towards 2 o'clock). There is a bunker on the left front and one on the right. Beyond the green is a big hill some distance away.

15.2 THE TEE SHOT. The challenge with the tee shot is to avoid being directly behind the evergreen trees. The ideal way to play this hole is to hit along the left side and let the gentle slope kick the ball back to the middle of the fairway. The ball is then far enough left so the evergreens do not block the approach. With the green being angled, approaching from the left also gives more green to work with.

The only other problem off the tee is the tee box itself. It is aligned to the right and is very uneven. I am careful not to align myself with the direction of the tee box and I spend the time to find a level spot.

15.3 THE APPROACH. With a reasonable drive I am usually around 110 to 120 yards (100 to 110 metres) from the middle of the green. I have a perfect lie and get aggressive.

When the pin is at the very back of the green I hit half a club more, or hit the shot with normal force rather than soft. With the green being angled, the exact distance to the back always seems to be further away than I think it is. The green holds well so I am not worried about going over.

The approach shot can be tricky with a headwind. Due to the hill behind the green, the headwind creates the wind shear effect. A strong wind can knock a shot down quickly.

When faced with wind shear, I hit a punch shot, aiming around the greenside bunker if it is in my line of play. In this way, even if the shot gets knocked down I am left with an easy chip or flip wedge shot rather than the bunker shot. Although I am a good bunker player I am slightly better with my chip and flip wedge shots.

This hole plays shorter than the distance on the card, mainly because it is downhill. Playing around the trees does not add an appreciable amount to the distance. If played correctly this hole is relatively easy and a definite birdie possibility. I expect to make 3 or 4 on this hole. A bogey is a bad score.

HOLE 16. PAR 3, 138 YARDS (126 METRES), HANDICAP 18

16.1 THE HOLE. The sixteenth is a short downhill par 3. The green is small and is surrounded by three bunkers, two at the front and another at the back left. Immediately to the left of the green is a small mound and further left a steep upslope with very long grass.

16.2 THE TEE SHOT. I discussed this tee shot in STAGE 4. Basically due to the unevenness of the tee box I frequently have a downhill lie off the tee. I adjust for this by using more club and swinging easy. I also aim for the middle of the green because the bunkers decrease the size of the landing area.

When this green is firm I purposely hit the shot into the mound to the left of the green and let the terrain kick the ball onto the green. I have seen a hole in one made in this manner (not mine).

16.3 ON THE GREEN. This is a good green to putt. The breaks are not big and the speed is consistent over the whole green.

This is a tricky little par 3 mainly because of the uneven tee. It plays about the same as the distance quoted on the card. I expect to make 3 or possibly 2.

I have also made a hole-in-one here. A smooth 8 iron.

165

HOLE 17. PAR 4, 415 YARDS (379 METRES), HANDICAP 2

17.1 THE HOLE. This hole is a dogleg left. Trees run the complete length of the hole on the left and further left is out of bounds.

17.2 THE TEE SHOT. As discussed in STAGE 5, I no longer attempt to drive over the corner trees. I now hit a 3 or 4 wood to the middle of the fairway.

17.3 THE APPROACH. The green is long and somewhat narrow. It has two tiers with a swale in the middle. There are bunkers to the right and left. Over the back is a steep downslope and dense bush.

My approach shot is usually 170 to 210 yards (155 to 190 metres). This green is a tough target to hit from this distance. I allow for the weather conditions and how far back the pin is and try to get the ball on or near the green.

This is a difficult hole for me. Because I hit a fairway wood off the tee I play it at its full length. I accept this added difficulty in order to reduce the probability of going out of bounds off the tee and scoring a double bogey or higher. I expect to make a par 4 or bogey 5. I play the hole conservatively and do not see birdie as a realistic possibility.

HOLE 18. PAR 4, 381 YARDS (348 METRES), HANDICAP 6

18.1 THE HOLE. The eighteenth is an uphill dogleg right. There are two fairway bunkers on the right in the tee shot landing area. The fairway slopes generally upwards and about 200 yards (180 metres) from the middle of the tee is a sharp upslope where the fairway rises to another level. This upslope is about 4 feet (1.2 metres) high.

18.2 THE TEE SHOT. This is another hole where the big hitters can drive past most of the trouble and have a short iron to the green.

How I play this hole depends on the tee position and the wind direction. If the tee is up front and there is a helping wind I can hit my drive far enough to fly the upslope in the fairway. This shot will then roll forward leaving a short iron in.

If the tee is in the middle or if I am hitting into a moderate headwind my normal shot will land into the upslope and get very little roll. In this situation I hit my driver hard trying to carry the swale. Should I happen to slightly mishit the hard driver the ball will probably land in front of the upslope and run through the upslope.

18.3 THE APPROACH. The green has three tiers and bunkers on each side. Immediately in front of the green is a steep slope which leads up to the front edge. A shot hit short into this slope will frequently kick into a bunker. As this green is normally firm, any shot landing on the green usually rolls to the rear.

Putting back down through the tiers is difficult because the swales are so steep the ball accelerates significantly as it passes over and down the swales. This can make it near impossible to get the ball close to the hole.

My target area for the approach depends on which tier the pin is on. If the pin is on the front tier, I play a run-up shot and make sure I do not hit the ball too far past the pin. I accept the risk of going in the bunker. If the pin is on the middle or top tier I try to land the ball on the green and accept having a downhill putt. I can handle putting through one of the swales, but not two.

This a hard hole to par. It plays much longer than the distance on the card because it is uphill all the way and the green is elevated well above the fairway. I am happy to make a 4 or 5 on this hole.

SECTION 16.1 — END OF HOLE BY HOLE ANALYSIS

These are the issues I consider when playing my home course. It took me years to learn the factors to watch for and how to adapt my game to the way the course plays. Even now, I know I can still make improvements in many areas.

At first reading the analysis of the factors stated may seem complicated. With me, they have become automatic. I set guidelines for each shot and remember the guideline. An example is with the tee shot on the first hole, I hit to the right side of the fairway. I then adjust this guideline based on the factors (weather, tee position, etc.) existing at the time.

I am totally convinced my detailed analysis of each hole has been a major factor in reducing my handicap. I suggest you apply the same detailed analysis to each hole at your home course. It is one way of reducing your handicap using a little common sense.

In one sentence, course management is the setting of your targets based on your level of skill.

SECTION 16.2 — TROUBLE SHOTS

This section covers trouble shots in general and provides some basic rules. Specific trouble situations were discussed throughout the hole by hole analysis in the previous sections of this chapter. I present trouble shots in this manner for clarity. Discussing a trouble shot on a specific hole and describing the complete situation puts the shot in the proper context and better communicates the concepts.

Learning to play trouble shots well directly affects your handicap. A good recovery shot will reduce the effect of a poor shot and may even negate the effect entirely.

My primary principle with trouble shots is damage control. I control the damage of the previous bad shot. I try not to lose any more shots by taking unnecessary risks. Miracle recoveries are rare.

The way I implement damage control is by going into defensive mode. This means I accept I am in a trouble situation and am unlikely to make a birdie. I try to save par if I can, but do everything to protect against a score worse than bogey. I can shoot 75 with a few bogeys, I cannot with a few triple bogeys.

When evaluating a trouble shot my priorities are:
1. If there is a danger of injuring myself or damaging my equipment I either chip out or take an unplayable lie penalty. No golf shot is worth this risk.
2. Get the ball out of trouble and back in play.
3. Advance the ball.
4. Put the ball in a good position for the next shot.
5. Get as near to the green as possible without risking going into a hazard or more trouble.
6. Get the ball on the green.
7. Get the ball in the best putting position.
8. Sink the shot (somewhat unlikely).

I set my goal for this trouble shot at the highest numbered item on the list that I feel I have a reasonable chance of accomplishing.

The factors to consider when evaluating trouble shots include:
1. Look at all options. Can I go over, under, around or through (gap) trees or bushes. Should I hit a shot left handed, use a putter, bounce the ball off a tree or a fence. Any option I can think of. Think, innovate, make up new techniques.

   Part of assessing these available options requires a detailed knowledge of your game. The things you need to know are:
   • The trajectory of a shot with each of your clubs. This includes the trajectory for a normal shot and any variations you can create. How high and how low, with adjustments can you hit each club.
   • How far can you hit each club. This includes swinging normally, hard, very hard, soft and very soft.

- How far can you intentionally hook or slice with each club and at what point in the trajectory will the curve begin.

You do not need to know exact numbers for all these factors but you should have a general idea. The more you know about your capabilities the more options you have and the more accurately you can assess these options. Learning your capabilities in these areas can take a considerable amount of time. It took me years.

2. Consider the consequences of a successful, a mediocre and a poor shot. Where is the ball likely to end up after these shots.
3. Avoid hitting the ball into more trouble at all costs. Avoid high penalty areas such as out of bounds, water hazards and dense bush. These almost always cost a full one shot and sometimes more.
4. Determine (or guess) your probability of success for the shot. I usually only consider options which I feel have at least a 50 percent chance of success. I determine this probability based on past experience and gut feel. After hitting a number of shots in similar situations I have gained a feel for whether or not I can hit the shot well, and whether or not it will be successful.

    Each person has to learn to assess each situation based on their own game. This takes experience. Until you gain this experience, think through the shot and make the best decision you can at the time.

5. I may attempt a shot with a less than 50 percent probability of success if I am in a desperate situation. For example, I am down in a match, playing the last hole and my opponent is on the green. Since I must win the hole I may decide to take a chance and hope for a miracle. I do not do this often.
6. If I am playing well I may choose a higher risk shot. If I am playing poorly I always choose a low risk shot.
7. Although I mentioned I play defensively, I do not play overly conservatively. I will take a chance if I feel I can save a par as long as there is a minimum penalty if the shot does not turn out the way I plan.

    I have seen a number of players chip out or lay up when I feel they should have tried to get the ball on the green. My assessment of the situation was the worst consequence they were facing was to have a slightly harder wedge shot. If they are a reasonable wedge player the risk is worth the gain of getting on the green. On the green they have a higher probability of saving par.

    I have seen too many lay up shots result in no real gain and many that cost one full shot.

I assess all the above factors and decide on my shot. Once I have decided on the shot I remind myself that I have made the best decision possible at this time. I do not want any doubt creeping into my mind when I am executing the shot.

Also remember hindsight is 100 percent accurate. Do not fall into the trap of questioning your decision process after a bad result. By all means check to see if you have not considered certain factors and if so, include them in your future analysis, but do not let low probability results affect your confidence.

Every shot has a probability of success and a corresponding probability of failure. When the result which had a low probability occurs, do not be surprised. If your analysis is correct this low probability result will only occur a low probability number of times. Or in other words, infrequently.

To summarize, with trouble shots think of all the possible options and the consequences of each. Avoid high penalty areas at all costs. Play to make bogey at worst. Minimize the effect of a bad shot by implementing damage control.

SECTION 16.3 — HOW TO PLAY A STRANGE COURSE

This section describes the adjustments I make when playing a course I have not seen before.

The first thing I do is go to the pro shop and get a scorecard. I prefer the scorecards that have diagrams of the holes and indicate yardages. The booklets with written suggestions for playing the hole are best. Such scorecards help me to play better and make the round more enjoyable. I wish every course had something for visitors. Even a one page map of the holes with some distance measurements would be useful. It would also help speed up play.

I then ask the people in the pro shop if there are 150 yard or 150 metre markers (to the middle of the green) and if so, which they are and how I identify them. Some courses have markers at the 150 yard point and some at the 150 metre point. Metres are approximately 10 percent longer than yards so I need to know which they are.

Generally my approach when playing a strange course is to be conservative. I try to drive down the middle of the fairway and play to the middle of the greens. I follow the contours of the holes and do not take shortcuts. I attempt to figure out how the course architect wanted the hole to be played and follow that route. When the architect has presented more than one route I take the conservative way. I do not expect to shoot my best score on a strange course. Because I do not know the course I find it easy to make double and triple bogeys. The main reason is I do not have the past experience with the course to know exactly how far I am from my target area and the hidden factors and hazards to avoid.

Examples are; how big a green is and where the ball will bounce when it lands on the green (or fairway), how close other trouble (bushes, water, etc.) is to the target area and whether the terrain will kick the ball towards this trouble, wet spots, special wind effects and other things mentioned throughout this book. To the uninformed, these all cost shots.

The following are additional factors I consider when playing an unknown course. They are general course management rules for playing par 3, par 4 and par 5 holes:

1. On a par 3, I look at the shape of the green and the hazards around the green. I will look at the pin position but this is secondary. On a strange course I normally just shoot for the middle of the green.

    I am concerned here about bunkers that cut into the landing area and arms of the green. I do not want to aim at a small target area. If the green is tiered or very large, I try to get my ball on the same level as the pin. If I can see the whole green and the target area is large, and it is a short hole, I will then, and only then aim for the pin.

    The distance on the scorecard is not always the distance the hole is playing. Sometimes tees are up front and sometimes they are back. The difference in the distance can be significant. Most courses have permanent markers somewhere on or near the tee indicating where the hole was measured. In some cases this is the sign for the hole, in others there is a marker on the ground. I use this permanent marker to pace off the actual distance to the tee markers and adjust accordingly.

    On these holes I will also watch which clubs my playing partners use. If I know the distances they hit their clubs I can use this information to help me in my club selection. I am careful to only note those shots that are hit well. A poorly hit shot should be ignored.

2. On a par 4, I try to determine the best place to hit my approach shot from and choose this as my aiming point for my drive. Things I watch for include hitting the ball through the fairway on dogleg holes, the placement of hazards and if there is out of bounds, how near it is to my target area. With all things considered I usually play to the middle of the fairway.

171

My general rule for club selection off the tee is if the hole is longer than 380 yards (340 metres) I use the driver. If the hole is shorter I carefully examine the width of the landing area and decide whether to use a 3, 4 or 5 wood. The narrower the area the higher the club I use. I handle my approach shots in the same manner as discussed in the previous point.

3. On par 5 holes, again, I usually end up aiming down the middle of the fairway. On a short par 5 I may decide to go for the green in two. If I think I can reach it I will usually go for it. This is a personal weakness of mine and one place where I violate my own course management rules. When playing on my home course I rarely go for a green in two, but on a new course I try it more often.

    I justify this by telling myself if I fail to get to the green and get into trouble, it is due to my unfamiliarity with the course. I then walk away happy. Remember my goal here is to enjoy myself, not shoot my best ever score.

4. When putting on a strange course I continue to play conservatively. I try to get long putts near the hole and do not make a major effort trying to sink them. My basic philosophy is to guard against three putting at the expense of making a few putts. The distance of the putt is more important than the direction.

    Prior to a round I always spend some time on the practice green. I get a feel for the amount of break and the general speed. For the first few holes I watch all putts, both mine and those of my playing partners. I use this information to determine the actual speed and amount of break the putts are taking.

At an unknown course I prefer to play the tees which are rated around 71. The courses, as they play at this rated level are usually enough of a challenge for me without being so difficult that I become frustrated and discouraged. I want to enjoy myself.

I have heard it said, by a non-authoritative source, that a single digit handicap player can expect to shoot at least two shots higher on a strange course. For higher handicap players it will be more.

In summary, when playing a strange course, play conservatively. Determine the routes the course architect has provided and choose the one you are most comfortable with. You are probably not going to shoot your best ever score so do not be needlessly aggressive. Play to avoid the double and triple bogeys, you can save more shots than you will probably gain. Think your way around the course, and above all enjoy the scenery.

CHAPTER 17
POTPOURRI

This chapter is a collection of issues and tips which do not fit into the other chapters but are relevant to the overall concept of this book.

SECTION 17.1 — RULES

The Rules of Golf are very complex and most people do not have the time or the interest to learn them in detail. However anyone who is serious about this game should have a general understanding of the rules. You need to know the basic regulations of the game you are playing.

To summarize the rules is beyond the scope of this book. I do however make some general comments on the rules and point out ways to use them to save shots. For more information I strongly recommend THE RULES OF GOLF Illustrated and Explained by Tom Watson with Frank Hannigan, published by Random House.

For the avid student I recommend DECISIONS ON THE RULES OF GOLF by the United States Golf Association (USGA) and the Royal and Ancient Golf Club Of St. Andrews (R&A). This is the official bible of the Rules of Golf. It lists over 1,000 specific situations and explains the ruling for each one. Almost every predicament that could occur in the game of golf is covered. This book is available from the R&A and the USGA.

When you discuss the rules with other golfers be careful with your choice of words. Many do not understand the rules and for some reason tend to get very emotional. Even if they are wrong and are proven wrong, many still are upset. I have seen some horrific arguments from normally calm people.

I have noticed most handicap players are reluctant to call penalties on others. Usually it takes something extreme before anything is said. This is good. We do not want the pleasant game of golf to degenerate into frequent arguments. Besides, if you regularly call penalties on people, you will get a reputation as a jerk and it may become difficult to find others who will play with you.

The advantage of knowing the rules is they will save you more shots than they will cost you. If you know the rules and use them to your advantage you can lower your scores.

The main area where benefits can be obtained is when taking free relief. If you know when you are entitled to relief and the relief procedure, you may in some cases be able to improve your lie and line of play.

In trouble situations the rules may give you more options than you are aware of. For example, once you have established your drop area you can then take the club-length(s) in any direction without going nearer the hole. You may be able to take trees and other objects blocking your shot out of your line.

Also remember with a drop, the ball can roll up to two club-lengths as long as it is not nearer the hole. In some situations you can use slopes in your drop area to cause your dropped ball to roll up to this two club-length limit. This again can improve your lie and line of play.

If your ball is in a water hazard you have three options (play it, replay shot or drop keeping point of entry between the point of drop and the pin) and with a lateral water hazard you have five options (the same three plus dropping within two club-lengths on either side of the lateral hazard). If you put a ball in water consider all the available options. Many players automatically reload and play again from the same spot. This is not required. By taking a drop near the hazard you usually gain some distance.

If you want to take an unplayable lie, you have three options (replay, two club-lengths no nearer and going back as far as you want). Again, knowing all the options for each situation and choosing the best one can save shots.

If you do take relief and gain a real improvement in your lie or line of play, do not let this bother you. I have seen players take valid free relief that got them out of trouble and then feel guilty. They then let this guilt affect their next shot. I have also seen knowledgeable people use the guilty ploy as a method of gamesmanship.

If you know you are entitled to relief take it, and do not feel guilty. There are times the rules give you good breaks and other times bad breaks. You have to accept the bad so you may as well accept the good.

Also be aware some people may question, to a point of yelling, whether you are entitled to relief. As I mentioned, many do not know the rules. Learn the rules well enough so you do not let an unknowledgeable person talk you out of relief you are entitled to.

On the greens watch for anything that can deflect the ball offline. You may repair ball marks as long as they are easily recognizable as ball marks. If in doubt consult your playing partners.

The Rules of Golf also allow you to repair unusual damage to the green.

Another area which can be helpful is advice. You can ask your caddie or partner anything but you are very limited in what you can ask an opponent or fellow-competitor. Examples of what you can ask an opponent or fellow-competitor are:

- Asking the distance of the hole, or the distance from a permanent object to the center of the green is allowed.
- Asking or answering the question of the distance of a ball (non-permanent object) to the center of the green is a violation.
- Asking the pin positions on subsequent holes is allowed.
- Looking in a players bag to see which club they are using is valid, however if the player has covered the clubs, for example by placing a towel over them, you may not move the towel.

Another area to watch for is Local Rules. A tournament committee may, although they do not have to, make Local Rules for relief from:

- Accumulation of leaves.
- Aerification holes.
- Unsurfaced roads.
- Stones in bunkers.
- Fixed sprinkler heads within two club-lengths of the green when the ball lies within two club-lengths of the sprinkler.
- Embedded balls through the green.
- Ant hills
- Edging grooves.
- Young trees.
- Apron or fringe of a wrong green.
- Balls lost in culverts or drainpipes.
- Unusual damage to course, for example areas where depressions exist or foot traffic has damaged the ground.
- A protective fence near the line of play, for example a fence that protects a teeing area.
- Ball deflected by power line.
- Uniformly poor course conditions (preferred lies).

I will take relief from these whenever I can. When in trouble I make an effort to look for free relief. Take advantage of the rules whenever you can. I am convinced knowing the rules helped reduce my handicap.

SECTION 17.2 — GOLF LESSONS

I believe lessons are useful, especially for learning the fundamentals of the game and the swing mechanics. As mentioned in Stage 1, I took lessons and found them worthwhile.

Choosing a teaching professional should be done carefully. There are many excellent teachers, but there are also a few bad ones. Before you take a lesson talk with the prospective teacher. Some professionals emphasize the feel of the golf swing and others are more concerned with the mechanics. Some follow a set methodology. Try to find one who communicates at the level you are interested in and uses terms and words you understand. This can be harder than it sounds.

I also believe that lessons only go so far. To be a good golfer you must be able to go beyond the lessons and this you must do yourself. By "going beyond the lessons" I mean you need to know your game and yourself (mental aspects) well enough so you are able to determine whether a tip is right for you and how to apply the tip to your particular game. Everyone is different and all tips are not for everyone. Reaching this level of understanding with your game can take years.

SECTION 17.3 — UNUSUAL HINTS

1. When thinking about your golf game remember things can be better, but they could also be worse. Look on the bright side. Count your blessings.
2. Golf is a game you play by yourself. This is one of the major attractions. You have no one to blame but yourself. This can be good and it can be bad.
3. I see from the professional tour statistics Curtis Strange averages 253 yards (231 metres) off the tee. Since he plays courses in the 7000 yard (6400 metre) range, I have always wondered if a person who hits the ball 10 percent shorter and regularly plays courses 10 percent shorter, is not playing under similar conditions. It sounds good but probably will not work out right.
4. On different days people are in different physical shape. One day they may be tired the next day not, or any degree in between. The shape they are in at the time affects their posture, reflexes, hand eye coordination and rhythm. To play well all the time you need to be able to adapt to these differences.

5. On the course be careful about picking up the tempo of your playing partners. If someone in your group is swinging very fast or very slow and you watch them, you may pick up their tempo subconsciously.

    Also be careful with putts. I have played with two golfers where I noticed a major difference. One player seemed to be hitting his putts very hard, long backswing and fast through the ball. When I watched him I tended to hit my putts too hard.

    The second player seemed to hit the ball ever so softly and it would roll and roll. When I watched him I tended to hit my putts too gently.
6. When your handicap is high your improvements are noticeable. When your handicap is low the improvements are not as noticeable.
7. When you are playing do not risk injury in any way. I once heard a story about a fellow who was killed making a shot. His ball had come to rest a few inches (centimetres) behind a tree root and as he swung at the ball the clubhead hit the root and the shaft broke. The bottom part of the shaft flew up and lodged in his neck. He died from the wound. Since hearing this I have been extremely careful.

    Also, never hit a shot into an area where there are people without first warning them. This includes hitting into the group in front, no matter how slow they are. Even if they are annoying you, it is not worth killing someone.

    Look for places on your course where shots tend to go. An example is where you walk back down the side of the fairway you have just played to get to the next tee. As you are walking watch the incoming approach shots.

    Be careful out there, there is more danger than people think.
8. Many years ago I read a statistic quoted by a course architect. Referring to the size of greens he said for every 75 yards (68 metres) the expected approach shot is from the green, the target should be 10 yards (9 metres) wide.

    So if a hole calls for an approach shot of 150 yards (135 metres) the green should be 20 yards (18 metres) wide. According to the architect this was a reasonable target area for a good player. The point is courses are built to allow for a certain amount of error.
9. I have one comment for greens superintendents. I have noticed the amount of criticism aimed at them is directly related to the critic's score. People who make high scores are more likely to complain than those who make low scores.

I suggest they not trick up the course if they want to keep the members from bugging them. This means setting reasonable tee and pin positions and cutting the fairways wide enough, perhaps even a little wider.

10. Learn the maintenance schedule of the course and play when the course is in the best shape. For example after the fairways are cut.

11. When I played golf in Las Vegas I noticed the greens were different in the way they accepted an approach shot. They had a sand base and when I walked on them they felt rock hard. However, when a full shot landed on the green the force of the ball would break the surface and the ball would check up well. A chip shot or partial wedge shot may or may not break the surface depending on the force with which the ball landed. It took a few shots until I was able to calculate which shots would break the surface and which would not.

12. When placing a tee in the ground be sure to use the ground, not the length of grass as a base for the height. The grass may not have been cut recently or different courses may cut the grass at different lengths.

13. When searching for your ball in the trees and bushes look in the clearings first. If you find your ball try to inform your opponent before you approach the ball. This reduces the chance your opponent will accuse you of moving the ball.

I was once playing a serious match and hit my ball into the bush. After we both searched for a couple of minutes I found the ball in a clearing with an open shot to the green. From my opponents reaction I was sure he thought I had moved the ball there. I won the match, but it was very close.

A few weeks later one of my friends mentioned he had heard my opponent making comments about me POSSIBLY moving the ball in the bush. He had not directly accused me of moving the ball, but implied I had done so. I chose to ignore his comments. Besides what can one do against innuendo?

Still this is something to think about. A person can get a bad reputation at their course if he or she is not careful. Many people are quick to assume others have done something wrong and spread stories around.

Along this same line, if your ball is in the bush and you want to take a practice swing be sure you take the practice swing some distance from the ball. If your opponent cannot see you, I suggest you tell him in advance you are only taking a practice swing. He or she will probably hear the club going through the bushes and assume you have taken a stroke at the ball and missed. I have seen this happen.

14. It is usually safe to assume an opponent who has a low handicap will take two putts or less from a medium distance, for example 20 feet (6 metres). If the opponent is a medium or high handicap player it is not safe to assume anything. I have seen an 18 handicapper take four putts from 10 feet (3 metres) in a big match. Do not take needless risks.

15. It is worth video-taping your swing and reviewing it every so often. You may be surprised at what you see.

16. An old golf adage is "You can only play with the game you have, not the one you would like to have". This point is made a number of times in this book but it is worth repeating. Accept your golf game for what it is at the time and take advantage of your strengths.

   If we all could play golf like the touring professionals we would all be on the tour. That is a different world from what the average handicap golfer sees. Do not make the mistake of comparing your game to theirs. Golf is their full-time job, it probably is not yours. How would your game be if you hit hundreds of practice shots most days and played almost every day?

   Also, do not be misled with the image of the touring professionals. Television coverage shows the professionals who are playing well that week. Those who are a little off are usually not mentioned. This creates the image in some people's minds that all tour pros are playing at the top of their form at all times. This is not true.

   If you get a chance to see scores from a number of rounds for most pro's you may be surprised with the number of scores over 75. No one can play at the top of their form all the time. A fact of the game of golf.

17. In a positive way, Jack Nicklaus and Greg Norman are freaks. They are exceptionally talented and can do things with a golf ball I can only dream of. Long ago I stopped attempting to reach their level.

18. I once shot a very solid round of 75. After this round I was convinced I had the secret of golf and would play great from then on. The next day I shot 96, yes 96, and almost cried. Golf is a humiliating game.

19. In a season where I play approximately 100 rounds I expect to have only four or five games where I play well in all areas. I may not score the best in these rounds but I know I have played well. These few are all I need to keep me coming back.

SECTION 17.4 — STORIES

1.   NEVER GIVE UP. When playing a match never give up. I was once three holes down with four holes left.

Standing on the 15th tee my opponent takes great pains to point out the status of the match. I just smile and ignore him. I win the 15th hole with a par and he is a little quieter. I win the 16th with a birdie and he is not saying too much. I win the 17th with a par out of a bunker and he is silent.

Standing on the 18th tee he laughs and makes a comment about how lucky I am to be one under par in the last three holes. I just shrug and say "The match is all square, right?".

My tee shot hooks into the trees. He laughs. I say nothing. His tee shot goes 240 yards (220 metres) right down the middle. Walking down the fairway he lets me know how easy this hole is going to be. I keep smiling.

I find my ball in the trees. I am approximately 180 yards (165 metres) from the middle of the green. The ball is sitting up well but I have tree branches about 20 feet (6 metres) in front blocking the approach. A stake for a planted tree is to the left of my line and I choose to ignore it. My problem is to get the ball on the green while staying under the branches.

From this lie I come to the conclusion the only club I can keep under the branches is a 3 wood, and I am going to have to hood it (close the face) to produce a low running shot. To get such a shot on the green from this angle is difficult. The green is elevated and the terrain slopes towards one of the bunkers. There is a very small margin for error.

So I pick my line, concentrate on keeping the shot low and hitting the 3 wood with about three-quarters force. I make a nice swing and hit the ball well.

WHAM! I have pulled the shot offline and hit the stake dead on. The ball dribbles back almost to my feet. There is loud laughter from the middle of the fairway.

I line up the shot again, this time ensuring I miss the stake, and hit a reasonable shot. The ball stays low under the branches and runs up towards the green. As it starts to climb the hill the slope causes it to go into a side bunker.

More laughter from the middle of the fairway. I clean my club and put it in my bag.

My opponent hits his shot to the front portion of the green. The pin is at the back and he has two tiers to negotiate.

At the green he looks at me and chuckles. He reminds me the match is all square and asks how many shots I have had. He knows I am three in the bunker. He points out he has only had two shots and is on the green.

I hit my bunker shot to about 5 feet (1.5 metres). This leaves me with a tricky sidehill putt. He hits his first putt just inside mine.

I spend extra time lining up my putt. I hit a good putt and the ball drops. My score is five.

My opponent now has to make his 4 foot (1.2 metre) putt to win the match. He lines it up carefully and strokes it. It does not even come close to the hole. He pulls it left about 3 inches (8 centimetres).

He is livid, swearing, swinging his arms. I concede his next putt. We are on to extra holes.

I walk ahead of him to the first tee (the extra holes start here). I let him think about his putt and what happened.

Off the tee I hit a mediocre drive down the middle, not long. He hits his tee shot 40 yards (37 metres) past me.

On the way to our balls he points out the difference in the distance of the drives. My only comment to him is "Gee, I was hoping I would play the last four holes one under par but just got a bad break on the last hole". In other words, I ignore his comment.

I hit my second shot slightly fat and the ball stops about 10 yards (9 metres) short of the green. My opponent hits his second shot into a bunker. I hit my wedge shot to about 10 feet (3 metres) and leave myself with a straight uphill putt (not intentionally, I was trying to get closer). My opponent hits a good bunker shot to about 6 feet (2 metres), but leaves himself a tricky sidehill putt.

I make my putt and he misses his. I win the match.

As I say, never give up. I was lucky to win this match but such things happen. By the way, the opponent took the loss very well after he calmed down. He is not a bad guy, just competitive. I do not believe his antics were designed to be gamesmanship, they were just his way of expressing himself under pressure.

2. A REAL TOURNAMENT. I do not remember the exact date but it was a few years ago and the last day for entries for the city amateur golf tournament, a big amateur tournament.

This tourney had three flights based on handicap, seven to nine, four to six and three and under. The highest handicap to enter was nine. A ten was just not good enough.

Playing in the city amateur had been a goal of mine for a number of years. At this time my handicap was ten and I accepted it. On this day I was hanging around the clubhouse and saw a notice on the bulletin board regarding the tournament. I did not think much of it at the time.

I then went to the handicap book and looked at my differentials. I suddenly realised by my calculations I had just made a nine handicap.

Click, hey I can now play in the city amateur! So I grab an entry form, rush to the pro shop and explain the situation. The professional tells me I must drop the entry off at the tournament office and have an hour to do so. I am elated. Finally I am a player. I have a single digit handicap.

Back to the clubhouse and up to the parking lot with my status symbol, an entry form to A REAL tournament. Well almost.

On my way to the parking lot I slip on the stairs in the clubhouse and break my foot. Yes, a crack in the bone, just behind my little toe on my right foot. So much for playing in the tournament.

As I look back on this I see it as funny, although at the time I did not. The doctor told me I would have to wear a cast from my toes to my knee for six weeks. This during the height of the limited golf season. Well, anyway I got my handicap down to nine.

Actually, while I was wearing the cast I had a look at my handicap calculations and found I had made a mistake. I was one shot over the range for a nine, therefore I was still a ten. All this for nothing. Well, I still believed I could become a nine handicap if I did not have this stupid cast.

So three weeks later I am at the doctor's office to get a walking cast put on. I ask him about playing golf and he said "No, too much walking". I mentioned I planned to rent a cart and ride around the course. He laughed and said "Sure".

At least I could play. One problem. A walking cast has a rubber tip on the bottom that will damage the greens by creating depressions when weight is applied to it. The greens superintendent pointed this out to me in a polite manner.

This was easily solved. I took an old running shoe and split the support behind the Achilles heel. This allowed me to get most of the cast into the shoe. I tied the laces around the back of the cast and above the instep which kept the shoe on and when I put weight on the foot, distributed the pressure across the bottom of the shoe. Therefore no damage to the greens. The greens superintendent approved. Off to the first tee.

Playing golf with a cast on one's leg is an experience. As I mentioned, the cast went from my toes to just below the knee on my right leg. The stub on the bottom of the walking cast made the right leg about 2 inches (5 centimetres) longer than the left leg. In order to hit the ball I had to make the following adjustments:

- At address, bending my right knee in at an angle of about 30 degrees.
- Taking a very slow backswing so I did not lose my balance.
- Stopping my backswing at three-quarters of normal because my hip turn was restricted by the angle of my right leg. This had an advantage in that I was able to create a lot of tension in my backswing with both my hips and upper body feeling some strain from the coiling effect.
- Aligning the ball off the toe of the clubface. As I started my downswing the uncoiling motion and the way I was balanced caused me to fall forward slightly. I hit a few shanks until I made this adjustment.
- Allowing my whole body to move left after contact with the ball. This was the only I way I could achieve any form of weight transfer. At the end of the swing the leg with the cast (right leg) would drag along the ground in the direction of my swing giving the appearance I was about to step forward. After this motion I had to be careful I did not lose my balance and fall over.

Overall, these adjustments were not hard to get used to. I found I did not play too badly and managed to keep my handicap at ten. If I can keep a ten handicap playing with a cast on my leg there is hope for everyone.

It is interesting to note my driving improved while playing with a cast. I started hitting the ball as straight as an arrow. I simply tried to get the ball in the middle of the fairway 210 yards (190 metres) out. Not trying for extra distance and not expecting too much seemed to be what I needed at that time. Many times I hit the ball well past my target distance. I have been unable to duplicate this level of accuracy since I had the cast removed.

All this hassle for my mistakenly believing I was eligible to enter a REAL tournament.

3. NO DOUBT. I once had an 8 foot (2.5 metre) putt to take a serious match into extra holes. There was no doubt in my mind I was going to make this putt. I read it to break 3 inches (8 centimetres) to the right just at the hole and hit it perfectly.

The putt did not break and went 6 inches (15 centimetres) past the hole. I simply could not believe this. I shook hands and thanked my opponent for the match. I then went back and hit the putt again. This time the putt broke and went in.

The message of this story is not every putt hit correctly goes in. Accept this and do not let such things shake your confidence. I still do not know what happened with the putt. Maybe the golfing gods kicked it out of the way. These things happen.

4.   IN THE END. As I think back over the thousands of shots I have hit, I am struck with a remark one of my golfing buddies once made. His comment was "In the end, all golf shots come down to some thought, some skill and some luck."

CHAPTER 18
ONE-LINERS

This chapter contains the main points discussed throughout this book in the form of one-liners. They are included to act as reminders for the reader and to allow a quick review of the information presented. They are listed in logical groupings and not in the order they were mentioned.

1. You are not trying to shoot 63, you are trying to shoot 75, occasionally.
2. The purpose of the game of golf is to get the ball in the hole in as few strokes as possible.
3. It is a myth that you need to hit the ball 300 yards (270 metres) off the tee, your wedge 130 yards (120 metres), make a lot of birdies and eagle all the par 5's to score well.
4. A shot saved is a shot saved no matter where it is saved
5. I can shoot 75 with a few bogeys, I cannot with a few triple bogeys.
6. The mental aspects can be far more important than the mechanics of the swing.
7. Identify the environmental factors that affect your golf game and make every reasonable effort to ensure they are met.
8. Poor off course preparation will affect on course performance.
9. Learn how to make short putts.
10. The ability to make short putts is the key to getting the ball in the hole, and getting the ball in the hole is the key to the whole game.
11. Learning how to make short putts reduces the pressure on every other aspect of the game.
12. If you keep the ball in play and can make short putts, the worst you should make on a hole is bogey.
13. Memorize (or make notes of) the breaks on the greens at your home course.
14. Plan your shots.
15. Realistically assess your strengths and weaknesses.
16. Course management is the managing of your individual game, with your strengths and weaknesses, around the course you are playing at the time.
17. Keep the ball in play.
18. Try to place every shot in the best possible position for the next shot.
19. Avoid major penalty areas at all costs (out of bounds, water hazards, dense bush).

20. A good recovery shot can negate the effect of a bad shot.
21. When in trouble, play to save par but more importantly, guard against more than bogey, implement damage control.
22. Take only reasonable risks but do not throw shots away by playing too conservatively.
23. Use routines to improve concentration and reduce the possibility of forgetting to consider all the factors necessary to hit a golf ball to the intended target.
24. Between shots, force your mind to think about the upcoming shot.
25. When preparing for the shot, mentally focus on your routines and checklists.
26. During the swing, mentally focus on your swing keys.
27. Try very hard on every shot.
28. I believe choking is caused by a loss of concentration and the loss of concentration is caused by insecurity and a lack of confidence.
29. If the concentration is regained the chance of choking is dramatically reduced.
30. You must truly believe that despite whatever realities the golf course will throw at you, you are a good player.
31. If you have hit a number of good shots you know how to hit good shots.
32. Hitting a few bad shots is part of the game.
33. When you do not play well look for the real reason, it may not be your lack of skill but due to a factor outside your control.
34. To quote from a famous speech by JFK "Some men see things as they are and ask why, I see things as they might be and ask why not?".
35. Set reasonable goals and objectives.
36. Listen to everyone, but only accept advice that you believe is valid for you.
37. Emotion, be it positive (elation) or negative (anger) is a part of the game.
38. Diffuse your emotions before you hit your next shot.
39. When faced with gamesmanship, realize it is an admission of weakness and try not to let it affect your game.
40. Choosing the proper home course will increase the probability of playing your best and having a lower handicap.
41. Learn the fundamentals of the swing (grip, address, etc.), this is the starting point for everyone.
42. Take lessons from a professional with whom you communicate.

43. Keep notes on regular problems that creep into your game, and include the remedies that were successful.
44. On the course watch for recurring problems and correct them when possible.
45. Develop a regular set of drills to help eliminate recurring problems.
46. Develop and use a pre-round warmup routine.
47. Practice occasionally.
48. No matter how much you practice and work there is a delay before the results become apparent, be patient.
49. As you improve in one area you put more pressure on another area of your game, which in turn has to be improved.
50. Exercise regularly.
51. Use the Rules of Golf to your advantage whenever possible by taking free lifts, etc. when entitled.
52. Get the right equipment for you, it will help you play your best.
53. If you wear glasses watch out for the distortion caused by the lenses.
54. If you are not aiming properly you cannot hit the ball to the target.
55. Determine the actual playing distance for a shot.
56. Learn the distances you hit your clubs, not including roll.
57. Think of what is going to happen to the ball after it lands.
58. Allow for the shot to be not hit perfectly.
59. Allow for the lie of the ball.
60. Learn how to adapt to different weather conditions.
61. Knowing the exact weather conditions will allow their effect on the flight of the ball to be predicted early in the round.
62. When starting a round in cool weather use one club more and in cold weather two clubs more, and swing easy.
63. On a very hot day hit one club less than normal and consider two clubs less.
64. When it is wet take one more club, swing easy, and do not try to hit fancy (curving) shots.
65. With a moderate headwind add one club, with a strong headwind take two clubs more.
66. With a strong headwind or angled wind consider hitting a punch shot.
67. Ignore a weak wind, or at the most make a small adjustment.
68. With a moderate or strong tailwind take one club less and allow for more roll.
69. With a crosswind adjust the target area by the amount you think the ball will be moved.
70. Watch for the funnelling, shielding and wind shear effects.

71. Time your shots to the gusts of wind.
72. Lighting conditions on a bright clear day are different than on a dull day.
73. When playing a strange course, play conservatively.
74. Be pleasant, positive and easy going on the course.
75. In the end, all golf shots come down to some thought, some skill and some luck.

CHAPTER 19
THE 19TH HOLE

To play well a golfer must learn to advance the ball, not long but a minimum distance, and keep the ball in play. He or she must also have a sound short game. These skills do not need to be at the level of a professional but at a reasonable level.

I believe the required expertise is far below most people's perceptions. I certainly did not reach the level I previously thought I had to.

Having these skills is not a guarantee of a good score, it is the beginning of advancing to the other issues of the game. These are the issues I have addressed in this book. They are as important, and I feel more important than the mechanics of the swing. These are the factors that allowed me to shoot 75, occasionally.

Generally, I attained this skill by analysing every factor, both on and off the course, that could affect my score. I tried every possible way to save a shot, improve an area of my game or reduce the problems I may experience.

I set up a strict regimen and made sure I stayed within this regimen (most of the time). I worked on and improved the all important mental aspects. I learned the effects of the various weather conditions and how to adjust to them. I taught myself how to consistently make short putts. I identified my recurring mechanical problems and the appropriate remedies. I learned how to apply my strengths and weaknesses to the playing characteristics of my home course. I gained the knowledge to implement the concept of damage control. I also searched for, and eventually found the right equipment.

In summary, I tried to improve not by spending hours on the practice range beating balls, but by analysing and learning the issues and factors discussed.

I wrote this book to show you the reader one person's experience and allow you the opportunity to learn from my effort. I hope that by seeing my approach you will recognize similar problems to what you are experiencing and gain some benefit. Perhaps this small contribution to your knowledge will allow you to love to love this terrible, exasperating, thrilling game. If so, my effort has been worth it.

As I mentioned in the opening chapter, should you find some of the factors and routines I discuss too detailed, I suggest you not try to apply them all at one time. Read them, select the few you feel will help you the most and work on integrating these into your game.

When you are comfortable you have incorporated your first selection, go back and select a second set. Keep selecting a few at a time until you feel you have mastered all the appropriate points. It took me many years to learn and integrate all the knowledge I have presented, perhaps you can do it in less time.

The ability to shoot 75 is an acceptable level. Touring professionals may not agree but I am sure there are many golfers who do. Once this level is reached, you can play with anyone at any time and be at ease with your game.

Golf is the greatest game I know. I remain and will always remain a student of the game. It simply fascinates me.

The feeling after a good round is impossible to describe but it is certainly one of the best feelings I know. I find there is simply nothing like it. Nothing. May you experience the same.

That is the story of how I learned to shoot 75, occasionally. The whole process took eleven seasons and my handicap dropped from 19 to 5. It required a lot of effort and work, but in the end it was all worth it.

No matter how badly I play in the future, or even if I never play again, I know, I was once A PLAYER.

Peace at last.

May your birdies be many and your bogeys few. Play well.

To Order

HOW I LEARNED TO
SHOOT 75, OCCASIONALLY

— A Fanatic's Approach To Golf

Please send $14.95 plus $4.00 postage
and handling to:

OZ IT
P.O. Box 51047
6525 - 118 Avenue
Edmonton, Alberta, Canada
T5W 5G5